D1361638

Physical Challenges

LIVING WITH A SPECIAL NEED

Attention-Deficit/Hyperactivity Disorder

Autism

Blindness and Vision Impairment

Brain Injury

Chronic Illness

Deaf and Hard of Hearing

Emotional Disturbance

Gender Issues

Intellectual Disabilities

Learning Disabilities

Physical Challenges

Protective Services

Speech Impairment

The Foster Care System

The Juvenile Court System

The Laws That Protect Youth with Special Needs

Physical Challenges

JOAN ESHERICK

MASON CREST

Mason Crest
450 Parkway Drive, Suite D
Broomall, PA 19008
www.masoncrest.com

Printed in the United States of America.

Series ISBN: 978-1-4222-3027-5
ISBN: 978-1-4222-3041-1
ebook ISBN: 978-1-4222-8826-9

Library of Congress Cataloging-in-Publication Data

Esherick, Joan.
  Physical challenges / Joan Esherick.
     pages cm. — (Living with a special need)
  Audience: Grade 7 to 8.
  Includes index.
  ISBN 978-1-4222-3041-1 (hardback) — ISBN 978-1-4222-3027-5 (series) — ISBN
978-1-4222-8826-9 (ebook) 1. Youth with disabilities—Juvenile literature. 2. Self-con-
trol--Juvenile literature. 3. Self-acceptance—Juvenile literature. I. Title.
  HV1569.3.Y68E924 2015
  362.4092'535—dc23
                                    2014010646

Picture credits: Artville: pp. 23, 38, 52; Autumn Libal: pp. 79, 80, 92; Benjamin
Stewart: pp. 20, 34, 40, 53, 94, 96, 105, 108; Corbis: pp. 36, 37, 50, 84, 106, 117;
Digivision: p. 48; Patricia Therrien: pp. 51, 78, 82, 95; Photo Disc: pp. 17, 19, 54, 55,
64, 65; Research Foundation/Camp Abilities: pp. 68, 70; Susquehanna Service Dogs:
pp. 22, 24, 56; Viola Ruelke Gommer: pp. 67, 116.

CONTENTS

KEY ICONS TO LOOK FOR:

Text-Dependent Questions: These questions send the reader back to the text for more careful attention to the evidence presented there.

Words to Understand: These words with their easy-to-understand definitions will increase the reader's understanding of the text, while building vocabulary skills.

Series Glossary of Key Terms: This back-of-the book glossary contains terminology used throughout this series. Words found here increase the reader's ability to read and comprehend higher-level books and articles in this field.

Research Projects: Readers are pointed toward areas of further inquiry connected to each chapter. Suggestions are provided for projects that encourage deeper research and analysis.

Sidebars: This boxed material within the main text allows readers to build knowledge, gain insights, explore possibilities, and broaden their perspectives by weaving together additional information to provide realistic and holistic perspectives.

A child with special needs is not defined by his disability. It is just one part of who he is.

INTRODUCTION

Each child is unique and wonderful. And some children have differences we call special needs. Special needs can mean many things. Sometimes children will learn differently, or hear with an aid, or read with Braille. A young person may have a hard time communicating or paying attention. A child can be born with a special need, or acquire it by an accident or through a health condition. Sometimes a child will be developing in a typical manner and then become delayed in that development. But whatever problems a child may have with her learning, emotions, behavior, or physical body, she is always a person first. She is not defined by her disability; instead, the disability is just one part of who she is.

Inclusion means that young people with and without special needs are together in the same settings. They learn together in school; they play together in their communities; they all have the same opportunities to belong. Children learn so much from each other. A child with a hearing impairment, for example, can teach another child a new way to communicate using sign language. Someone else who has a physical disability affecting his legs can show his friends how to play wheelchair basketball. Children with and without special needs can teach each other how to appreciate and celebrate their differences. They can also help each other discover how people are more alike than they are different. Understanding and appreciating how we all have similar needs helps us learn empathy and sensitivity.

In this series, you will read about young people with special needs from the unique perspectives of children and adolescents who are experiencing the disability firsthand. Of course, not all children with a particular disability are the same as the characters in the stories. But the stories demonstrate at an emotional level how a special need impacts a child, his family, and his friends. The factual material in each chapter will expand your horizons by adding to your knowledge about a particular disability. The series as a whole will help you understand differences better and appreciate how they make us all stronger and better.

—*Cindy Croft*
Educational Consultant

YOUTH WITH SPECIAL NEEDS provides a unique forum for demystifying a wide variety of childhood medical and developmental disabilities. Written to captivate an adolescent audience, the books bring to life the challenges and triumphs experienced by children with common chronic conditions such as hearing loss, intellectual disabilities, physical differences, and speech difficulties. The topics are addressed frankly through a blend of fiction and fact. Students and teachers alike can move beyond the information provided by accessing the resources offered at the end of each text.

This series is particularly important today as the number of children with special needs is on the rise. Over the last two decades, advances in pediatric medical techniques have allowed children who have chronic illnesses and disabilities to live longer, more functional lives. As a result, these children represent an increasingly visible part of North American population in all aspects of daily life. Students are exposed to peers with special needs in their classrooms, through extracurricular activities, and in the community. Often, young people have misperceptions and unanswered questions about a child's disabilities—and more important, his or her *abilities*. Many times, there is no vehicle for talking about these complex issues in a comfortable manner.

This series provides basic information that will leave readers with a deeper understanding of each condition, along with an awareness of some of the associated emotional impacts on affected children, their families, and their peers. It will also encourage further conversation about these issues. Most important, the series promotes a greater comfort for its readers as they live, play, and work side by side with these individuals who have medical and developmental differences—youth with special needs.

—Dr. Lisa Albers, Dr. Carolyn Bridgemohan, Dr. Laurie Glader
Medical Consultants

Words to Understand

 handicapped conversion van: A van that has been specially adapted to pick up and carry a wheelchair. It often has been modified to include a lift.

lift: Mechanical or electric ramp or platform that can be raised or lowered.

service dog: A dog that has been trained to help people with various disabilities.

physical disability: A condition that causes a person to have difficulty with seeing, hearing, walking, talking, climbing stairs, lifting, carrying, or performing activities of daily living.

activities of daily living (ADL): Feeding, grooming, dressing, bathing, writing, using a keyboard or telephone, etc.

severe disability: Unable to see, hear, walk, talk, climb stairs, lift, carry, or perform activities of daily living independently without the help of another or without the use of assistive technology.

assistive technology: Methods or equipment used to help people with disabilities perform ordinary tasks and become more independent.

assistive technology devices (ATDs): Equipment used by people with disabilities that helps them perform ordinary tasks and become more independent.

physical challenges: Disabilities involving movement or manual function.

spina bifida: A birth defect in which the spine doesn't close and the spinal cord is vulnerable to injury. This condition often results in paralysis.

cerebral palsy: A condition characterized by brain injury before, at, or shortly after birth that results in abnormalities of muscle tone and coordination.

1

A New Neighbor: Meeting Someone with Physical Challenges

Samantha rifled through the pile of letters and magazines she held in her arms as she rushed inside from her trip to the mailbox. Ah! It was there. Her monthly issue of *Yo, Girl!* magazine had arrived. Dumping the rest of the mail on the kitchen table, she hurried to her bedroom, closed the door, and plopped stomach-first onto the double bed that dominated her room.

Is it here? She wondered, her heart thumping in her chest. She flipped through the magazine's glossy pages. In a matter of moments her eyes spotted the column she sought: "Dear BJ: Awesome Advice by and for Teens." Scanning the letters that made up this month's advice column, she looked for a familiar signature. There it was! In print! Her very own letter! The letter she'd sent three months ago when she found out her best friend and next-door neighbor was moving away.

Dear BJ,

I don't know what to do. I just found out that my best friend, Ali, is moving! Her dad got a new job in another city about a thousand miles away. Our parents say we can still see each other a couple times a year—you know, like at Christmas and over summer vacation and stuff, and we can IM each other on the Internet. But it won't be the same. I mean, Ali lives right next door and we do everything together. What am I going to do? She can't move! We've been very best friends since we were little, and she's the only true friend I have. Nobody understands like she does. Help!

Signed,
Sad in Cincinnati

Samantha felt a renewed ache in her heart as she read her own words. Three months ago, her best friend was only *going to* move. Now she was gone. The vacant house next door with the "SOLD" sign out front confirmed her new reality. What would BJ say? What *could* she say? Nothing would bring her best friend back.

Dear Sad in Cincinnati,

Losing your next-door neighbor is going to hurt, and hurt a lot. Don't feel bad about being sad. It's okay to be sad. You're facing a big loss. You can try to keep the friendship going over the long distance, but the friendship will change. You are right to expect that it will be different, because it will.

My suggestion would be to keep in touch with Ali, grieve her absence, too, but allow room in your heart for the possibility of new friends. You have another kindred spirit living out there somewhere; I know you do! She may be someone you already know but never considered because of how close you and Ali have been. Or she may be a stranger, someone who has yet to enter your life. As someone once said, "Strangers are only friends we haven't met yet." So grieve your loss; you're entitled! But be alert for new friends. They're out there! I just know they are.

Yours truly,
BJ Twiam

How can I be alert for new friends when I miss the old one so much? Samantha thought after she read the reply. Maybe this time BJ Twiam really didn't understand.

Samantha closed the magazine and put her head down on her arms. The revving of an engine and the pulsing "beep" of a large truck backing up interrupted her grief. Samantha wiped her face with her sleeve, sat up, and pushed the sheer curtain aside that covered her window. A moving van was pulling in next door. The new neighbors were moving in!

"But she's in a *wheelchair*, Mom!" Samantha protested when her mother insisted they go over and welcome the new neighbors. Samantha had spotted special equipment when it was unloaded from the moving van. She'd also seen the new girl get out of her parents' **handicapped conversion van** by using a motorized platform, called a **lift**, to lower the teenager out of the van.

So much for finding a new friend next door, Samantha thought as she observed the neighbors' arrival. *Ali and I used to play basketball on that driveway. We used to roller blade there and toss lacrosse balls in the yard. We ran track together and swam together. Who am I going to find to do all that with now?*

"I think you should go over with me, just to say hi," Samantha's mother encouraged. "Who knows? Maybe you'll have more in common with their daughter than you think."

Yeah right.

"C'mon, Sam. We'll just run this plate of cookies over and introduce ourselves. It'll be fun. I really think you should come with me."

"Okay," Samantha sighed. "But only because you say so." She didn't want to go. She missed Ali, and the last thing she needed was to meet the people who were replacing the neighbors she'd had all her life. She wanted to stay away.

Samantha didn't know what to expect when she and her mother visited the neighbors, but she certainly didn't anticipate what she found when they arrived. The house next door, *Ali's* house, wasn't the same: new ramps led to the front porch; a wider door had been installed. All kinds of changes had been made to the place.

What happened to the old door? Sam wondered when her mother knocked. Where was the door Ali and Sam had used almost daily for a decade, the one marred by a dent in the middle where Samantha had accidentally driven a lacrosse ball? She couldn't resist peeking through the window at the top of the new door. Everything inside looked different, too. Boxes were piled floor to ceiling, fresh paint covered the walls, hardwood and tile floors replaced the old wall-to-wall carpeting, and the hall seemed wider, too. The new owners had done quite a bit of remodeling on the house before they moved in.

Samantha's thoughts came quickly as she waited. *It doesn't even look like Ali's house anymore. It doesn't smell like her house. What did they do to this place? I just want Ali to live here again!*

"Hi, I'm Maggie Stevenson," Samantha's mother introduced herself when the door opened. "And this is my daughter, Samantha. We live next door and just wanted to welcome you to the neighborhood."

A brunette, forty-ish woman with kind eyes stood in the doorway. Dressed in sweats with a towel thrown over her shoulder, she looked like she could have just come from the gym. She'd been unpacking instead.

"Well, ah, thank you! What a nice surprise. Oh, I'm Donna Vanderhoff, and that's my husband, Rick, over there," she replied gesturing to the tall man who stood behind stacks of boxes in the adjoining room.

The family seemed pleasant enough. They were excited to learn that Samantha and their only child, a daughter named Jenny, were the same age and would be in the same classes at school. The adults chatted a bit, and Samantha learned that Mr. Vanderhoff's company had transferred him—the same reason Ali's family's had to move. The new neighbors had more in common with the previous owners than Samantha realized: Mr. Vanderhoff even coached basketball in their old town—something Ali's dad had done.

That's odd, Samantha thought. *Why would he coach basketball when his only child uses a wheelchair?*

A bounding golden retriever startled Sam out of her thoughts.

"She won't hurt you," a laughing voice called as its owner wheeled around the corner into the foyer. Samantha saw a fit-looking girl with long, straight blonde hair rolling toward her. Her poise and easy manner immediately attracted Samantha.

"Her name's 'Giddy,' short for Gideon, which was the name I'd already picked out when I thought I was getting a male ***service dog***. When she arrived and we found out she was a girl, we just called her 'Giddy' instead. Oh, and I'm Jenny—Jen. I was just out walking Giddy. It's nice to meet you." Jenny extended her hand.

Walking Giddy? How can someone in a wheelchair walk a dog? Samantha was confused, but politely introduced herself. Then, not wanting to intrude further on their neighbors, Samantha and her mother excused themselves and turned to leave. As they said their goodbyes, Sam noticed the top of a familiar magazine sticking out from a large cloth pocket attached to the back of Jenny's wheelchair. It was her favorite, the one in which she'd just read her letter: *Yo, Girl!* magazine.

Maybe she and Jen had something in common after all.

HOW MANY PEOPLE HAVE CHALLENGES?

- The U.S. Census Bureau estimates that one in five Americans has some kind of **physical challenge** (*difficulty* seeing, hearing, talking, walking, climbing stairs, lifting, carrying, or performing **activities of daily living (ADL)**.
- One in ten is estimated to have a **severe disability** (*unable to* perform the activities listed in the preceding paragraph without the help of other people or from **assistive technology**).
- For children between the ages of six and fourteen, the U.S. Census Bureau estimates that physical challenges may affect as many as one in eight.
- The U.S. Centers for Disease Control and Prevention's (CDC) National Center for Health Statistics (NCHS) estimates that in 2011, over seventy-four million Americans had activity limitations.
- The NCHS found in 1994 that 7.4 million Americans used **assistive technology devices (ATDs)** to help them get around (walk, stand, use a wheelchair, etc.).

SOURCES OF PHYSICAL CHALLENGES

People become physically challenged three ways:

1. They are born with **physical challenges**. These challenges may arise from a problem with how a baby forms in the womb or an event that happens while the baby is still forming or while it is being born. The problems may be obvious at birth, such as limb abnormalities or **spina bifida**, or they may take time to diagnose, such as cerebral palsy, because the problem is with the central nervous system.
2. They develop a disease or condition that results in

physical challenges. Muscular dystrophy, multiple sclerosis, arthritis, diabetes, cancer, spinal meningitis, stroke, and other illnesses and conditions can cause physical disabilities.

3. They sustain an injury. Accidents, near drownings, poisonings, falls, sports, fires, and violence can all result in injuries that cause lifelong disabilities.

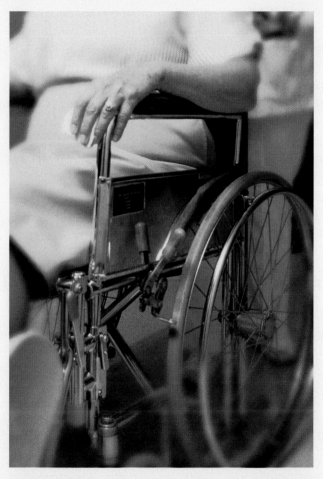

A person with a physical disability must often use a wheelchair.

MEDICAL CONDITIONS THAT CAN RESULT IN PHYSICAL CHALLENGES

cerebral palsy
spina bifida
muscular dystrophy
traumatic spinal cord injury
stroke
traumatic brain injury
arthritis
diabetes
polio
Parkinson's disease
amyotrophic lateral sclerosis (ALS; Lou Gehrig's disease)
multiple sclerosis
heart and lung disorders
Lyme disease
other neuromuscular disorders
other skeletal disorders
spinal muscular atrophy
meningitis

SPECIAL EQUIPMENT USED BY PEOPLE WITH PHYSICAL CHALLENGES

People with physical challenges often use special equipment, called assistive technology devices (ATDs), to help them do everyday things. ATDs come in as many varieties and complexities as the people who need them. Here are just a few:

- Wheelchairs, walkers, crutches, or canes help people walk or get around.
- Electric lifts carry wheelchairs in and out of motor vehicles or up and down stairs.

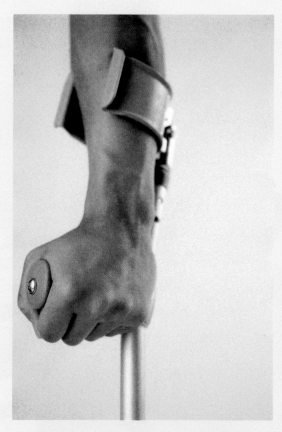

Crutches are one form of ATD.

- Braces or splints stabilize muscles to make it easier to do certain tasks.
- Communication devices allow a person to "talk" by pushing keys or picture squares on a lapboard or computer keyboard. The device "speaks" for the person.
- Voice-activated computers provide computer access to people who can't use their hands.
- One-handed computer keyboards make keyboarding possible for those who can use only one hand.

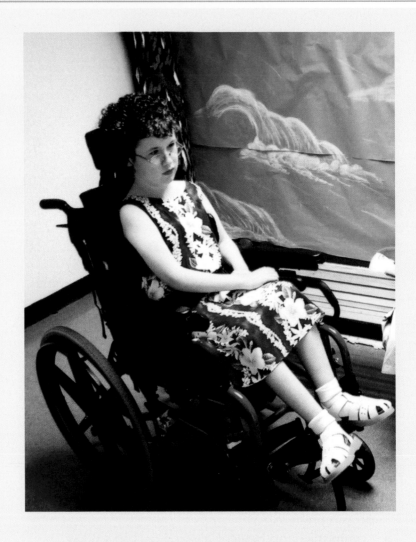

COMMON REACTIONS TO PEOPLE
WITH DIFFERENCES

Samantha's reaction to Jenny's wheelchair use illustrates a common response to people with differences. Despite great gains in understanding and acceptance in society, people in the disability community still face these common responses:

- Awkwardness: "I don't know what to say." "What could we have in common?"
- Fear: "What if I say the wrong thing?" "What if he has a seizure or something?"
- Pity: "I really feel sorry for her." "It's too bad that she can't do so many things."
- Embarrassment/Shame: "She's not like everybody else." "I don't want to be seen with her."
- Frustration/Anger/Resentment: "I don't care if he's physically challenged, he just better not inconvenience me." "Why should she get preferential treatment?"
- Discrimination: "If he's physically handicapped, he must also be mentally handicapped, deaf, incapable, or unable to make his own decisions."

How People with Physical Challenges Can Handle Reactions

1. Try not to take it personally. That may be difficult at first, but most fear or awkwardness comes from ignorance. People react to disabilities the way they do because they don't know any better.
2. Treat people politely and with patience.
3. Ignore teasing or bullying. If you feel threatened, report it or get help.
4. If you're being overlooked or ignored (e.g., a waiter at a restaurant asks your friend what *you'd* like to order), speak up!
5. Be an educator. Inform people about your condition. Do a report or presentation in class. Offer to be interviewed for your school or local paper. Talk honestly, without embarrassment, when people ask you about your condition. Volunteer information. The

more at ease you are with yourself, the more at ease people will be with you.

6. Be as independent as possible. Do as much for yourself as you can. Only ask for help when you really need it.

7. Show genuine interest in others' interests, activities, and feelings. Don't only talk about yourself. Try to find things you have in common.

8. Know your rights! Don't be afraid to appropriately cite the Americans with Disabilities Act if you find your rights being violated. (See page 117.)

A service dog can open doors for a person with physical disabilities.

Make Connections:
Watch How You Say It!

Don't Say:	Do Say:
Crippled, lame, or handicapped	Physically challenged or differently-abled
Confined to a wheelchair	Uses a wheelchair or is a wheelchair user
Victim of, suffers from, or is afflicted with a disease or condition	Lives with or has a disease or condition

Research Project

Use the Internet to find out more about how service animals can help people with physical disabilities. How are they trained? Be sure to read about other service animals besides dogs.

Service dogs can do many things to make their owners' lives easier.

WHAT CAN SERVICE ANIMALS DO?

A service animal is an animal that has been trained to help someone with a disability perform everyday tasks. Most people are familiar with guide dogs that assist the blind, but service animals can be other animals (like monkeys or even miniature horses) and can do many things. Service animals aid their physically challenged owners by:

- retrieving or picking up dropped items.
- helping them walk.
- helping them keep their balance.
- opening doors or cabinets.
- turning on wall-mounted light switches.
- carrying items in a small pack.
- carrying items by mouth.
- pulling wheelchairs.
- helping owners get up if they fall.
- sensing and then alerting owners and caregivers to oncoming seizures.
- helping owners undress or dress themselves.
- hearing and alerting their owners to sounds the owner cannot hear.

Text-Dependent Questions

1. If you had a group of sixteen children, how many would be likely to have physical challenges?
2. What are three ways someone might end up with a physical challenge?
3. Describe three types of special equipment that might be used by people with physical challenges, besides a wheelchair.

Words to Understand

wheelchair basketball: An adapted version of regular basketball played much the same way except that participants play from their wheelchairs.

spastic: Having tight, rigid, or stiff muscles.

diplegic: Having to do with weakness affecting both legs.

degenerative: Tending to get worse.

paralysis: Loss of function or sensation in a part of the body; can be partial or complete.

orthopedists: Doctors who specialize in treating disorders of the bones, joints, skeleton, or muscles.

neurologists: Physicians who specialize in the nervous system and its disorders.

physical therapists: People who are trained to help patients improve their large muscle skills, including walking, rolling, standing, using a wheelchair, and using crutches.

occupational therapists: People who are trained to help patients improve their fine motor skills and become more independent with activities of daily living.

speech/language pathologists: People trained in helping patients form words, speak, or communicate orally.

ophthalmologists: Doctors who specialize in eye disorders, injuries, and conditions.

prosthetists: People who study, design, and fit artificial limbs.

2

CEREBRAL PALSY: SURPRISED BY JEN

Samantha spent the next few days hiding out in her room. School was closed for Easter break, and she didn't feel like doing anything with anyone over vacation. A week didn't give her enough time to visit Ali, and that was the only thing she really wanted to do.

Mrs. Stevenson nagged her daughter to get out and enjoy the beautiful spring days, but Samantha was too sad and lonely. She lived for that hour in the evening when her parents allowed her to IM her long-distance friend. But Ali hadn't been on-line as much lately. She had things to do with her new friends.

Samantha stretched out on her bed and leafed through several back issues of *Yo, Girl!* Then she reread BJ's reply to her own letter of this month's issue. "Another kindred spirit. . . . Be alert for new friends." It seemed like Ali was making new friends. Why couldn't she?

I just don't want new friends. No one can be a friend like Ali.

The sound of a basketball on concrete pulled Samantha away from her thoughts. She hadn't heard someone playing basketball outside since Ali moved away. Peeking through her curtain, she saw her new neighbor, Jenny, in her wheelchair, dribbling the ball. While Samantha watched, Jenny started to move around the concrete court. She bounced the ball once, then put the ball in her lap and pushed her wheels' hand rims forward, then dribbled again. Next, Samantha saw her pop a wheelie and tightly pivot her wheelchair to get in better position to shoot. With perfect arm form,

Jenny propelled the ball toward the ten-feet tall hoop. Swoosh! Nothing but net.

Samantha was too curious to stay inside and watch. She had to talk to this girl.

"Where'd you learn to shoot like that?" Samantha called to her neighbor as she approached the driveway where Jenny practiced.

"Oh, hi, Samantha!" Jenny answered. "Just around, I guess. I played in a junior **wheelchair basketball** league in my old town. You guys don't have anything like that here, do you?"

"I don't know. But Ali and I, uh . . . the girl who used to live in your house, played in a basketball league for girls. Her dad was the coach."

"Really? My dad used to coach our junior wheelchair team. Wheelchair basketball was a pretty big thing in Charlotte. That's where I moved from."

Samantha noticed Jenny's mild Southern accent for the first time. Her drawl betrayed that she'd lived in the South for a while, but probably hadn't been born and raised there.

"You want to shoot a while?" Jen offered the ball to Samantha, who took the ball hesitantly at first. But once her hands felt its familiar tread and her arms fell into the familiar up-and-down pattern of bouncing the ball, she relaxed. Basketball seemed to break the ice.

The two girls spent the afternoon shooting and dribbling and talking together. Jenny could sink the ball every bit as well as the people on Samantha's old team. Even as well as Ali. And from her wheelchair, she could bounce pass and chest pass and dribble with the best of them. Sam noticed that Jenny's legs, which seemed smaller than the rest of her body, were strapped together in the chair. There were braces around the backs of her legs and ankles. Samantha wondered if her neighbor could move them.

"I have **spastic diplegic** cerebral palsy. CP for short," Jenny volunteered when she noticed Samantha staring at her legs. "It's okay, you can look. Lots of people do."

Samantha's face flushed. "I'm sorry. I didn't mean to."

"It's okay, really. I'm used to it." Jenny's ease amazed Sam.

"What's spastic dipleee . . . whatever you just said?"

"Spastic diplegic cerebral palsy. It's a condition that happens for lots of reasons. With me it was because my brain didn't get enough oxygen either before or while I was being born. It affects the part of the brain that makes you able to move and control your muscles. In my case, just my legs are affected; that's what 'diplegic' means. 'Spastic' means that my muscles are tight. Some people have a form of CP where their muscles are too loose."

"Will it get worse?"

"No, it's not ***degenerative***, but it won't get better, either. It's a permanent condition. I've been this way since I was born." Jenny seemed so casual about it.

"So are you paralyzed or something?" Samantha figured she'd better ask now while they were on the subject. Jenny didn't seem to mind answering.

"Oh, no. I don't have ***paralysis.*** I can still feel things in my legs, and I can move them. I can even walk with a walker or crutches. My legs are just really weak, and the tendons behind my ankles have gotten so tight that my toes point down when I'm not wearing my braces. I can't lift my toes or control my legs well enough to walk long distances or run. I use a chair for sports; it's the only way I can participate. And I use a chair when my legs are super tight or sore, or when I'm really tired. But I can get around pretty well with forearm crutches for short distances."

Samantha didn't quite know what to say. Jenny seemed completely at ease discussing her condition.

"You're pretty good with that thing," Samantha complimented Jenny, nodding toward her chair.

"You have to be if you want to play in a wheelchair league. You have to have all the basic skills down first, like popping wheelies and pivoting and stuff. I've been playing for four years now, so my skill is improving. I have to practice my drills, though, just like any other basketball player."

Samantha identified with Jenny's attitude. It seemed like they had more in common than she'd guessed at first.

"So, what other things do you like to do?" Samantha asked as she plopped into the grass next to the driveway where Jenny sat rolling her chair back and forth.

"I like other wheelchair sports, like hand cycling. And I like writing. I used to work on my school's newspaper, and I hope to do that here. And I like to read, you know, like books and magazines and stuff."

"Yeah, I saw *Yo, Girl!* in the pouch of your chair the other day when my mom and I stopped over. I like that magazine, too."

Jenny cocked her head to one side and grinned. "I saw your letter in this month's issue."

"Wha . . . how'd you know it was my letter?"

"Oh, let me see, hmmmm. The letter was signed, 'Sad in Cincinnati.' Where are we? Cincinnati. Neighbor's name was 'Ali.' Your old neighbor's name was 'Ali.' Neighbor's father got a new job; Ali's dad got a new job. I just guessed."

"Okay, already. It was mine," Samantha admitted.

"So what'd ya think of BJ's reply?" Jenny asked with genuine interest.

Sam wasn't sure how to answer.

"It was okay, I guess. Normally I really like how she answers in her column. I feel like, in some weird way, she understands things. But this time, I don't know. She got the part right about how much I'd miss Ali, but I think she blew it on thinking I'd be able to find a friend like her again."

Now it was Jenny's turn to flush. "I think she was probably just trying to encourage you," Jenny replied quietly, defending the columnist. "She may know more than you think."

"Yeah, well what could she possibly know?" Samantha's voice betrayed more emotion than she wanted it to.

"Well," Jenny seemed to be searching for words. "She probably knows what it's like to lose a friend or to move away. You don't know. She could have been through the same thing. Maybe she knows that it's possible to make new friends, even when your best friend moves away. Maybe she knows you just have to give people a chance."

"Oh well, it's just a stupid column anyway," Samantha sighed. "And I'll bet she gets paid to write it. She probably doesn't even care about the people who write the letters."

Jenny disagreed. "I think she does. I think she cares a lot, or she wouldn't be doing a column. Writing's not that easy. Believe me, I know."

"Hey, Beege!" Jenny's dad called from the front door. "Don't you have to get ready for your staff meeting?" His interruption diffused their rising emotions.

"Beege?" Samantha looked at Jenny quizzically.

"It's my dad's pet nickname for me. Nobody else uses it. Beege is short for 'BJ,' which is short for 'Beautiful Jenny,' which is what Dad called me all the time when I was little. 'My beautiful Jenny.'" Jenny rolled her eyes in an only-parents-can-embarrass-us-this-way look, and then tossed the basketball to Sam. She started rolling herself across the driveway.

Samantha's mind started racing. *BJ? Likes to write? No . . . it can't be. Not the same BJ. No way!* She could feel a knot growing in her stomach.

"What's the staff meeting thing?" Samantha persisted.

"Well, remember I told you I wrote for my school newspaper?" Jenny called as she rolled up the ramp to the porch. "I write for some other things, too, and once a month we do a teleconference, you know, like a meeting by phone, just to talk about what we're working on." Jenny stopped at the top of the ramp and looked back.

The knot in Samantha's stomach clenched tighter still. "That wouldn't be a magazine, would it?"

"Well, as a matter of fact, it is."

"But not, *Yo, Girl!* right? I mean you're not *that* BJ, are you?"

Jenny looked at Samantha, a mischievous gleam in her eye. "BJ Twee-uhm, at your service," Jenny said with her best southern drawl as she bowed with a flourish.

Samantha was mortified. "But, BJ Twiam? That's not your real name!" she blurted. "What does it mean?"

"It's not 'beautiful Jenny' anymore. I changed it to '*Beautiful Just The Way I AM.*'" Then Jenny turned and rolled her chair through the door.

WHAT IS CEREBRAL PALSY?

CP describes a set of conditions and symptoms that result from damage done to the brain usually before, during, or shortly after birth. The involved person's muscles and nerves are fine, but damage to the part of the brain that controls motor function makes it difficult for a person with CP to control movement.

- CP has a wide range of causes, including abnormal formation of the brain prior to birth, lack of oxygen, bleeding problems in the brain, and infection.
- CP is a permanent, chronic condition; it lasts for life.
- CP is not degenerative; the condition does *not* get worse over time.
- CP is *not* a disease or illness, and it is not contagious.
- There is no cure for CP.
- In some cases, head injury or trauma can cause a person to acquire CP later in life.

STATISTICS ON CEREBRAL PALSY

According to the CDC:

- Approximately 10,000 babies born each year have or will develop cerebral palsy (CP).
- Eighty percent of people with CP developed the condition before birth, at birth, or within one month after birth.
- About 50 percent of people with CP use braces, crutches, walkers, wheelchairs, or other adaptive equipment to help them walk or move around.
- Nearly 70 percent of people with CP have other disabilities, including learning disabilities and intellectual disabilities.

- On average, when researchers compared CP to seventeen other birth defects, it cost more to care for a person with CP from birth to death than it cost to care for an individual with any other birth defect in the study, including spina bifida and Down syndrome.
- The National Information Center for Children and Youth with Disabilities estimates that between 500,000 and 700,000 Americans have CP.

A student with CP may use a special computer.

TYPES OF CEREBRAL PALSY

CP is classified several ways: by degree of disability (mild, moderate, or severe), by type of CP (how CP affects the muscles), and by what part of the body is involved.

Degree of Disability:	Mild	Moderate	Severe
	Results in general clumsiness and poor balance	Results in uneven gait, limping, tripping, and possible need for leg brace or cane	Most physical abilities affected; results in the need for a wheelchair or other devices
Type of CP: (can have a mixture of these three types)	Spastic Marked by muscles that are too tight and stiff; high muscle tone	Athetoid (dyskinetic) Marked by involuntary movement and variable muscle tone	Ataxic (rare) Marked by poor balance, poor coordination, hand tremors, and difficulty with depth perception
Parts of the body affected:	Diplegia Involving primarily the legs	Hemiplegia Involving only one side of the body (one arm and leg)	Quadriplegia Involving all four limbs and possibly the trunk and face

DOCTORS AND OTHER PROFESSIONALS WHO HELP PEOPLE WITH DISABILITIES

A person with CP or other physical disabilities may need to see these specialists:

- **Orthopedists:** physicians who specialize in treating problems with bones and muscles.
- **Neurologists:** physicians who specialize in treating nervous system disorders.

- **Physical therapists:** trained specialists who help patients improve their gross motor skills and become more independent with movement (sitting, standing, walking, rolling, using a wheelchair or crutches, etc.).
- **Occupational therapists:** trained specialists who help patients improve their fine motor skills, especially hand strength and function, and who help patients become more independent with ADL.
- **Speech/language pathologists:** trained specialists who help patients with communication skills, especially pronunciation, understandability, and clarity.
- **Ophthalmologists:** physicians who specialize in treating the eye and its disorders.
- **Prosthetists:** specialists in the design and fitting of braces and artificial limbs.

A physical therapist helps patients improve their ability to move their large muscles.

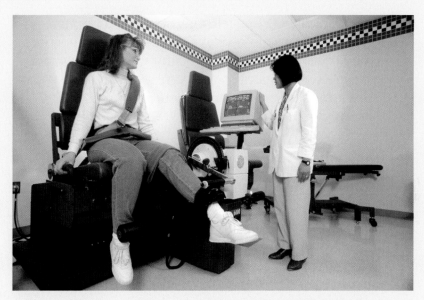

Various types of equipment may be used to improve the mobility of patients with CP and other physical disabilities.

HELP FOR CP

While doctors cannot treat the brain injury that causes CP, they can do much for its resulting symptoms. Here are just a few of the treatment and assistance options available to someone with CP:

- physical, occupational, and speech therapies
- orthopedic intervention (braces, splints, casts, shoe inserts, etc.)
- surgery (to release tight tendons, lengthen tight muscles, realign bones, etc.)
- assistive technology (communication devices, adapted keyboards, computers, etc.)
- adaptive equipment (Velcro closures for clothing, modified chairs, etc.)

- mechanical aids (wheelchairs, forearm crutches, walkers, etc.)
- medications (muscle relaxants for tight muscles and muscle spasms; anti-convulsants to control seizures; other medications to reduce jerking or muscle twitches, etc.)

COMPETITIVE SPORTS FOR WHEELCHAIR ATHLETES

archery	basketball
fencing	power soccer (motor soccer)
rugby	shooting (air rifles)
skiing	sledge hockey (ice hockey on sleds)
swimming	tennis
table tennis	track and field
volleyball	water skiing
weight lifting	

Sports Recognized by the International Paralympic Committee

Summer Sports	Winter Sports	Wheelchair Sports
archery	Alpine sitskiing	wheelchair basketball
basketball	Alpine skiing	wheelchair curling
Boccia	curling	wheelchair dance sport
bowls	ice sledge hockey	wheelchair fencing
cycling	ice sledge	wheelchair rugby
equestrian	speed racing	wheelchair tennis
football,	Nordic sitskiing	
five-a-side	Nordic skiing	
football,		
seven-a-side		
goalball		
judo		
powerlifting		
sailing		
shooting		
swimming		
table tennis		
volleyball		

COLLEGE STUDENT WITH CP SWIMS LAKE ERIE

On August 31, 2002, twenty-year-old Canadian Terri-Lynn Langdon swam twelve miles (19.2 km) across Lake Erie from Sturgeon Point, New York, to Crystal Beach, Ontario. Amazingly, the young athlete completed this swim using primarily her arms. Diagnosed with spastic diplegic CP, her legs could only contribute 10 percent to her swimming effort. The crossing took her twelve hours and fifty-five minutes: she averaged fifty-six to sixty strokes per minute, and maintained a pace of one mile per hour (1.5 km/hr).

Swimming helps improve the muscle tone of individuals with physical disabilities.

Research Project

Wheelchair Athletes Worldwide is an organization that donates sport wheelchairs to athletes with physical challenges. Go to their website to find out more about this organization:

http://wheelchairathletesworldwide.org/content/index.php/about

Describe the four founders of the organization. Why did they start their organization? What is their mission?

Terri-Lynn's accomplishment not only raised public awareness of CP but also raised nearly $15,000 for the Ontario Federation for Cerebral Palsy. Perhaps even more, she showed the world just how much someone with physical challenges can do.

Text-Dependent Questions

1. What are some of the things that could cause cerebral palsy?
2. What are some of the other disabilities that many people with CP have?
3. What are some sports that wheelchair athletes can play?
4. Why was it amazing that Terri-Lynn Landon could swim twelve miles?

Understanding banishes prejudice and judgment.
—Eliza Penn

Words to Understand

prosthesis: A man-made, artificial replacement for a lost body part.

amputee: Someone who has lost a limb through surgery or traumatic injury.

special education: Learning strategies tailored to fit unusual needs.

hemiplegia: Paralysis on one side of the body.

paraplegia: Paralysis of the lower limbs and lower half of the body.

quadriplegia: Paralysis in all four limbs and trunk.

head stick: An assistive technology device that resembles a headband from which a stick-like pointer protrudes. The user wears the head stick and moves his head forward and back using the stick to type or press buttons, etc.

voice dictation: Technology that allows a person to operate a computer or word processor by only using his voice.

3

Not All Disabilities Are Alike

"I can't believe I said those things to her, Mom." Samantha confessed later as they worked on making a salad for dinner. "I mean I told her I thought that the person who wrote those columns didn't really care and that I didn't like her answer to my letter. How was I supposed to know that the columnist was really Jenny, or BJ, or whatever she calls herself?"

"You couldn't have known, and Jenny was probably just looking for honest feedback."

"Well I gave it to her all right." Sam ripped a lettuce leaf viciously. "At least the stuff about her reply. That was honest. But the stuff about BJ not caring, that was just mean. I guess I was missing Ali and didn't know what else to say." Samantha threw the last of the lettuce into a salad bowl and started carrying it to the table.

"Look," Mrs. Stevenson turned and stopped her daughter, gently taking the salad bowl and setting it on the counter. Covering Samantha's hands with her own, she said firmly, "How long have you told me that you really liked this writer's column in the magazine? You've told me over and over again how much you identify with what she says and how much she seems to understand things. And now you find out that the columnist you like so much lives right next door! She hasn't changed, Samantha. She's still the same person. You two can actually get to be friends."

"Not now. Not after what I said to her." Samantha dropped her gaze to the floor. "I can't look her in the face again."

"Sure you can. Just go over and talk to her." Her mother squeezed Samantha's hands.

"But, Mom," Samantha started to whine when the telephone's ring cut her off. "I'll get it." She pulled her hands from her mother's grasp and reached for the receiver.

"Hello, Stevenson's."

"Samantha? Is that you?"

"Yes, this is Samantha. Who's this?"

"It's me, Jenny, from next door. Can you come over tonight? I have a proposition for you." Jenny seemed cautious, but excited.

The knot in Samantha's stomach came back. "Well, ah . . . , okay, I guess. What time?"

The girls set a date for seven o'clock. Samantha wondered what exactly Jenny meant by a "proposition."

Giddy barked as Samantha knocked on her neighbor's front door.

It's not a bad door, I guess. Just different. Samantha caught herself thinking about the girl who used to live there, and the changes that had been made to the house. Surprisingly, thoughts about Ali didn't hurt so much this time. Maybe the changes weren't all bad.

Jenny answered the knock on her feet this time. Samantha was startled to see her neighbor standing before her, leaning heavily on crutches. Jenny was nearly as tall as Samantha, but not quite.

"Hi, Samantha! C'mon in," Jenny invited.

Samantha followed the other teen through the foyer and kitchen into the family room. *This doesn't look like Ali's house anymore,* Samantha thought as she followed her neighbor. *It looks like someone else's house. It is someone else's house now.* She was so consumed with the changes to the house that she barely noticed Jenny's awkward gait as she walked with her crutches.

The two teenagers paused when they entered the room. "Welcome to my space," Jenny nodded toward the far end of the family room. "Or maybe I should say, BJ Twiam's space."

A long, wide desktop sat in the corner. A computer, piles of letters and papers, and large manila envelopes crowded the workspace, along with a dictionary, thesaurus, and other reference books. The area beneath the desk was wide open and clear. In front of the desk sat Jenny's wheelchair. Unpacked boxes filled the other end of the room.

Placing her crutches in the space between the desk and the wall, and leaning on the desktop, Jenny smoothly swung herself into her wheelchair. It was a different wheelchair than the one Sam saw her neighbor use playing basketball. This one had higher sides and the wheels were straighter; the wheels of the other chair were angled out. Samantha noticed a thick cushion on the seat. It looked comfortable.

"You seemed pretty surprised this afternoon when you found out I was BJ," Jenny said to Samantha as she turned on her computer.

"Well, uh . . . yeah. I guess I was," Samantha replied as she lowered herself into the overstuffed chair on the far side of the desk. "But, hey, I really didn't mean what I said about you, er, I mean, BJ, not caring. It was a stupid thing to say."

"No. It was honest. It wasn't all true, but it was honest." Jenny seemed unruffled and poised. She always seemed that way. She turned toward Samantha and continued. "You don't know me, Sam. And I'll never be Ali; I don't want to be. But I do care. Really. It's why I do this. And I do it because it's something I *can* do. My disabilities may keep me from doing some things other girls do, but I know I write well. At least that's what my teachers and parents have told me for a long time. So when I had the chance to try out for the teen columnist's position, I jumped at it. My parents thought it was a great idea, and I had nothing to lose. So I went for it, and got the job. It's not as glamorous as it seems, though. And it doesn't pay much. It's fun, and I feel like I'm helping people, but it's a lot of hard work." Jenny patted the stack of letters on her desk.

"Are all those from your readers?" Samantha asked.

"Yep, and I have to read every one and decide which to answer in the magazine each month. I try to answer them all anyway, but only a few get published."

"So why'd you pick mine?"

"Because you were genuine. You were honest. And I really did understand what you were going through. I was moving, too, you know."

Sam noticed a trace of sadness in Jenny's voice.

"Anyway, the reason I called was because of something that came up at the telephone meeting I had this afternoon. My editors asked me to write a real article for the magazine. Not just my normal teen column but an entire feature! I've never done a whole article before, so this is pretty scary. Exciting, but scary." Jenny grinned, but Sam saw that her smile wobbled a little.

"Scary? But you seem so confident."

"Well, don't believe it. My stomach's been doing somersaults since I got off the phone. So, anyway, the article's supposed to be about teens with physical challenges, but my own story can only be part of it. I need to find stories about other teens who have different disabilities. I don't know anybody here yet, except you. And I figured since you've been here all your life, maybe you'd know some kids I could interview. Would you be willing to help me? Maybe we could do the story together?"

Samantha's heart flickered with excitement. Or was it hope? Whatever it was, it felt good.

"Wow. No one's ever asked me to do something for a magazine before! Well, uh, yeah, I guess I could help. I know this guy in my algebra class who had his leg cut off in a lawn mower accident when he was little. He wears a fake leg. Would that count?"

"It's called a **prosthesis**, and that means he's probably an **amputee**. And sure, that counts. Maybe you could introduce us when I start school with you next week."

"And my mom's friend is a ***special education*** teacher at the high school. Maybe she could help us find some others."

"That'd be great. I really appreciate it." Jenny's gratitude was sincere. "Oh, and one more thing," Jenny continued. "Do you think I could interview you, too?"

Jenny's question confused Samantha.

"Well, uh . . . why? I don't have any disabilities."

"It's usually good to get other views on things," Jenny explained. "Like, in this case, it would add a lot to the article to know how people who don't have disabilities view people who do. The only way we can know is to ask."

Samantha squirmed as she recalled her reluctance to meet her new neighbor. "I don't know. Can I think about it? I'm not sure I'd be very good."

"You'd be great, but don't worry about it. We can decide later. I just really like your honesty and think you'd make a good subject. Right now, we need to find some other kids to interview. My friends from the basketball league in Charlotte are too far away. I'd like to do this up close and personal." Jenny grinned again, and this time her smile didn't waver.

"This is so cool. I can't wait to get started, Jenny."

"Me, too," Jenny agreed. "But call me, Jen. My *friends* call me Jen."

MYTHS ABOUT PEOPLE
WITH PHYSICAL CHALLENGES

MYTH: All people who use wheelchairs use them all the time.
FACT: Some people use wheelchairs all the time, but others use wheelchairs only for certain activities. These people may use crutches, canes, or walkers the rest of the time.

MYTH: People with physical challenges are mentally challenged, too.
FACT: While some may be, many people with physical challenges are not mentally, psychologically, or emotionally challenged.

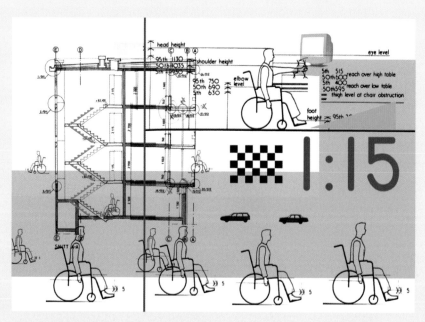

Adaptations to buildings, vehicles, and furniture allow individuals with physical disabilities to live active professional and personal lives.

MYTH: People who use wheelchairs wear "diapers."
FACT: Many wheelchair users have normal bladder and bowel function. As long as a bathroom is accessible (can fit a wheelchair, has handrails next to the toilet, etc.), these people can use the bathroom much like anyone else.

MYTH: People with physical challenges don't date or get married.
FACT: Most people with physical challenges have the same desires as their able-bodied friends: They want to be loved and accepted, they want to be attractive to others, they want and are able to experience sexual intimacy, and they may want to marry and have kids.

HOW FAMILIES REACT TO YOUTH WITH PHYSICAL DISABILITIES

Jenny's parents focused on her abilities and supported her when she wanted to try new things (like applying for the "Dear BJ" position). Their acceptance, love, and support modeled healthy responses to a loved one with physical challenges. Some families respond in unhealthy and damaging ways:

Some are overprotective: Though well intentioned, these families feel like they must do everything for the family member with a disability. They worry constantly and discourage risk taking or attempting new things.

Some fall into despair: These families view their loved one's situation as all bad and completely hopeless. They stop trying to make progress and are often sad.

Some get angry: These families resent how disability disrupts their lives. Instead of seeing their challenged family member as a person, they see him as an obstacle to happiness. These families may withdraw emotionally from their family member and provide only minimal care for him. They

Various professionals can help families and individuals learn to cope when a family member has a physical disability.

often make the affected person feel guilty by blaming him for his condition.

Counseling and support groups can help families overcome these less-than-ideal reactions.

DI, HEMI, PARA, OR QUAD?

Physical challenges can affect the entire body or just certain parts. Medical specialists refer to areas of involvement in different ways:

- **Diplegia**: when paralysis affects the legs.
- *Hemiplegia*: when paralysis affects one side of the body, including one arm and leg on the same side of the body.

- **Paraplegia**: when paralysis affects the lower half of the body, including both legs.
- **Quadriplegia**: when paralysis affects all four extremities, the body, and sometimes the face. Quadriplegia is also referred to as tetraplegia.

The "plegias" listed above can be "complete" or "incomplete." These are words typically used to refer to spinal cord injuries.

"Complete" describes when all sensation and motor function is lost. A complete quadriplegic has lost all ability to feel or use his arms and legs.

"Incomplete" describes when only partial sensation and motor function is lost. For example, an incomplete quadriplegic has paralysis in all four limbs and body, but retains some sensation and partial movement.

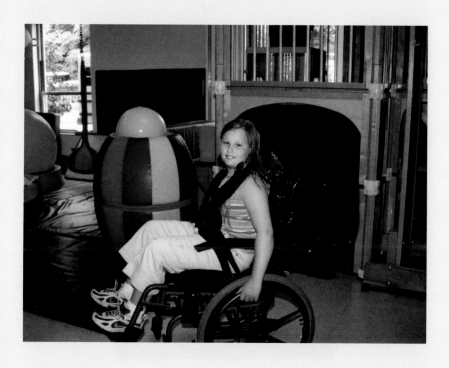

Make Connections: Jobs for Everyone

With the exception of jobs requiring physical labor, people with physical challenges can do just about anything:

People with quadriplegia find work as artists (using mouth sticks and pencils), illustrators, vocal musicians, composers, writers (using a *head stick* for keyboarding or *voice dictation software*), counselors, actors, motivational speakers, and much more.

People with diplegia have gone into broadcast journalism, computer programming, architecture, graphic design, data entry, research, teaching, lab analysis, Paralympic sports, and virtually anything else that does not depend heavily on using your legs.

People with hemiplegia have pursued retail work, educational fields, editing, customer service, human resources, business management, software design, sales, journalism, and any other job that can be performed with one hand.

With the assistive technology available today, those with physical challenges can pursue educational and vocational opportunities like never before.

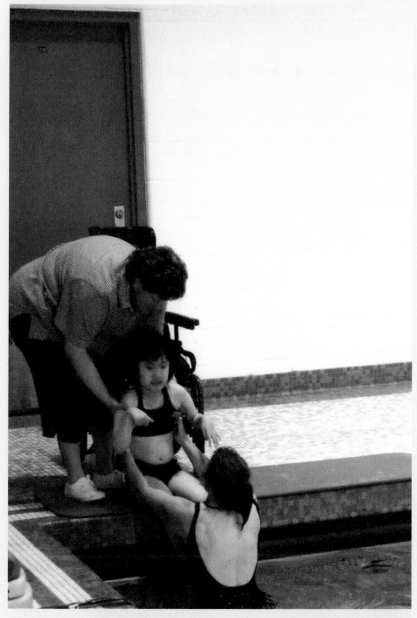

Individuals with physical disabilities are capable of excelling in many areas, including sports.

WHEELCHAIRS

Different Types

Wheelchair users have many choices when deciding which wheelchair to buy:

- Weight: Ultralight, lightweight, and standard cover are the available options. Adult-size wheelchairs can weigh as little as fourteen pounds.
- Design: Collapsible frame or rigid frame? Tilt wheels or straight wheels? High back or low back? Titanium frame or alloy frame? Armrests? Side guards? Sided foot rests?
- Wheels: Coated or uncoated hand rims? X-core wheels or spox wheels? Street tread or all-terrain tread? Shock-absorbing suspension or no suspension?
- Seat: Sling seat or molded cushion seat? Twelve-inch seat depth or twenty-inch seat depth? Foam seat cushion or pressure-relieving cushion?

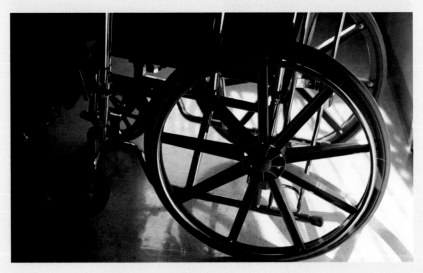

Wheelchairs come in many forms.

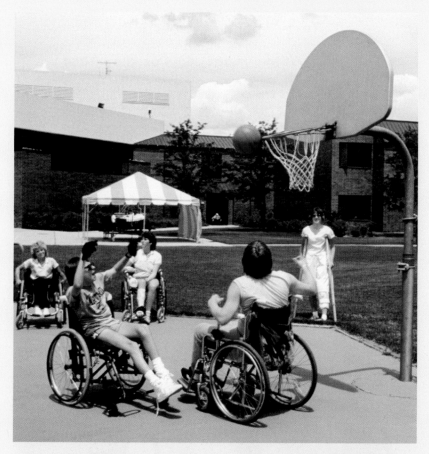

These individuals in wheelchairs enjoy a game of basketball.

Wheelchairs can be custom built to fit the user and his purposes. Manufacturers even make special wheelchairs for basketball, tennis, road racing, and other sports.

Basic Wheelchair Moves

To be independent and to participate in wheelchair sports, a wheelchair user must know these basic skills:

Text-Dependent Questions

1. List four myths about people with physical challenges. Explain why each one is not true.
2. How is hemiplegia different from paraplegia?
3. Why is a "wheelie" an important move for wheelchair users?

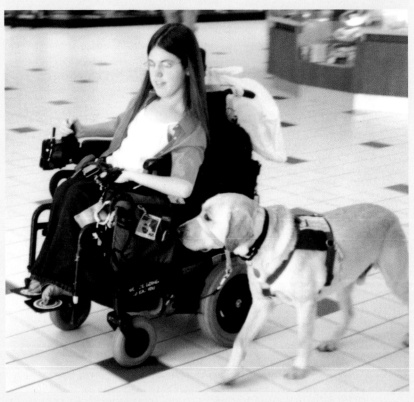

This service dog is trained to accompany his owner as she navigates her wheelchair.

- Lateral transfers: moving from the wheelchair to a bench, bed, or chair, and back again.
- Floor transfers: getting into the wheelchair from the floor, in case of a fall.
- Forward propulsion: rolling the wheelchair forward in a controlled fashion.
- Backward propulsion: rolling the wheelchair backward in a controlled fashion.
- Turns: turning the wheelchair left or right with control.
- Wheelies: tipping the wheelchair backward to lift the front wheels (called castors) off the ground. This is essential for moving over short obstacles like street curbs.
- Pivots: doing sharp turns in tight spaces without backing up.

Research Project

Some people with physical challenges participate in extreme wheelchair sports. Use the Internet to find out more about this form of extreme sports by answering the following questions:

- What are some specific challenges that these athletes have?
- How many different kinds of extreme wheelchair sports can you find? List them.
- What kind of equipment is use by mountain bikers and off-roaders with physical challenges?
- How can a person with physical challenges go downhill skiing?
- What kind of physical strength and ability do these sports require?

By having faith . . . you can overcome whatever challenges you face in life.
—Todd Huston

Words to Understand

amp: Slang for amputee.
stump: The part of a limb that is left after amputation.

4

AMPUTATION:
AN INTERVIEW
WITH TYRONE

"Jen," Samantha said, "this is Tyrone. Tyrone, this is Jenny Vander-hoff, a.k.a. teen columnist extraordinaire from *Yo, Girl!* maga-zine."

The three teenagers sat at a table in the school cafeteria—Jenny in her wheelchair at the head of the table, Samantha and Tyrone at opposite sides on round table-attached stools. The building had long since emptied; most kids either had gone home or attended af-ter-school practices. The cafeteria echoed with occasional sounds of custodians cleaning up or of a few isolated students cutting through on their way to the gym or rehearsal rooms. Tuesday afternoon after school was a great time for the interview.

"Wow. You mean you really write for a magazine?" Tyrone looked impressed.

"Sure do!" Jenny replied as if she'd answered that question a thousand times before. "And it's nice to meet you."

"Oh yeah, nice to meet you, too."

"Now Tyrone, I think Samantha's already filled you in on the details, right?" Jenny checked the clipboard she held in her lap.

"Sure. Yeah, um, she said you wanted to talk to me about my leg."

"Well, we're doing an article about teens with disabilities, and I wanted to get some ideas about what it's like to live with different kinds of challenges. What I live with having CP might be different than what you live with as an amputee."

Tyrone nodded and glanced down at Jenny's strapped-in legs. She was using her wheelchair today.

"To make sure we get it right, and to make sure I quote you correctly, I brought along a mini cassette recorder. Is it okay with you if I record our interview?"

Tyrone glanced at Samantha and shrugged. "Sure, I guess. Do I have to talk loud or something?"

"No, a normal voice is fine." Jenny set the tape recorder on the table between them and pushed "record."

"Let's get started then. Samantha and I prepared a list of questions, and I guess we can take them one at a time. Okay?"

"Shoot," Tyrone answered, glancing at the tape recorder.

"First, a little background. Tell us about your disability. What is it, how long have you had it, and how did you get it?" Jenny's professionalism impressed Samantha.

Tyrone took a deep breath, as if to calm his nerves, then jumped in. "Ah, well, let's see. I'm an LBK amputee. That means 'left below the knee,' and I've been an LBK *amp* since I was three years old. I'm fourteen now, so it's been eleven years." Tyrone seemed to relax once he started talking about himself.

"How did you lose that part of your leg?" Jenny prompted.

"I think I was running after a ball or something. Whatever I was doing, I slipped on the grass and slid under the lawn mower as my dad rode by. We have a big yard, and my dad was using a riding lawn mower. I was pretty little and my leg just slipped underneath. Anyway, before Dad could stop the blades, my foot and lower leg got caught. The docs couldn't save my foot and ankle, there was too much damage, so they amputated a few inches below my knee."

Tyrone swung his left leg up and plunked it on the table. He rolled up his pant leg to show the two interviewers where his leg ended and the prosthesis began. Like Jenny, he seemed completely at ease with his differences. Samantha didn't quite know what to think.

"What's been the biggest challenge for you since you lost your lower leg?" Jenny continued. She didn't skip a beat and paced her questions well.

"Phantom pain." Tyrone answered without any hesitation, rolling his pant leg down and pulling his leg off the table. Samantha was surprised. She expected to hear him say something about the things he couldn't do or how people reacted to him. She was becoming increasingly aware of her own misconceptions when it came to disabilities. First Jenny, now Tyrone. Neither was what she expected.

Jenny kept the interview moving. "What is phantom pain? Can you tell us more about it?"

Tyrone shifted in his seat. "After you lose a limb, it's like your body still thinks the limb is there. Like, I still feel pain in my left foot, which seems impossible because I don't have a left foot anymore. Sometimes it hurts and sometimes it itches."

"You mean your **stump**?" Jenny asked, looking for clarification.

"No, I mean my foot. Sure my stump hurts sometimes and it itches sometimes, but I actually feel pain and itching where my foot and ankle used to be."

"What causes phantom pain?"

"Nobody quite knows for sure. Doctors can't really explain it. Some say it's because the nerves at the end of the stump, where the amputation took place, grow back or are hypersensitive. Sometimes it's because surgery wasn't done right. For those cases they have to do surgery again. Others say it's because not enough blood gets to the injury site. That's why exercise helps; it increases blood flow through the stump. But nobody really knows for sure. All we know is that the pain is real."

"So what do you do for it? The pain, I mean."

"Sometimes I wear a special sock over my stump that's supposed to protect the nerve endings. But mostly, I exercise. If it really gets bad, my doctor prescribes pain medication that helps."

"What kind of exercise do you do?" Jenny continued. Samantha's interest peaked at this question. What could someone with a prosthetic leg do? She didn't know Tyrone well. She barely saw him at school, and she had no idea what kind of activities he was into.

"I like to run, actually. And I like to swim."

"You're a runner?" Samantha cut in. It was the first thing she'd said since the interview started. She couldn't hide her surprise.

"Sure. Amputees can do just about anything anybody else does. We just do it differently. Like running. I might not be as fast, but I can run. And I run pretty well. Good enough to make the track team. I have a special prosthesis I use for running. It's different than this one." Tyrone gestured beneath the table.

Samantha was beginning to realize that a world of disability or, rather, a world of *able* people with challenges, existed that she knew nothing about. She might be helping Jenny by arranging the interviews, but Jenny, she realized, was really helping her.

"Is there anything else you'd like to add, Tyrone?" Jen sounded like she was wrapping up the interview.

"Not really. Except that I really don't look at myself as disabled. I'm just another teenager, like every other teenager. I just don't happen to have a foot. That's all."

Jenny reached over and turned off the tape recorder.

"So, how'd I do?" Tyrone asked the teen columnist as she completed her notes on his last comment.

"You did great! You really seemed like yourself and you seemed comfortable enough. That's what I was looking for. I think there's a lot I can use here for our article. What did you think, Sam?"

Samantha didn't know what to say. She was still getting over her shock that Tyrone was a runner. "Well, uh, yeah. It sounded good." She looked at Tyrone and then she blurted, "I didn't know you could do stuff like that."

"You just have to give people a chance, Sam. Take some time to get to know us." Tyrone and Jenny exchanged glances. The two teens who'd only just met seemed to share an unspoken understanding.

"Yeah, I guess you're right," was all Samantha could manage to say. Jenny had said the same thing to her the other day. Maybe her words held some truth.

"Hey, well thanks a lot. I really appreciate your help on this," Jenny offered her hand to Tyrone. They shook, and Tyrone pushed himself up from the table.

"Anytime. Glad to do it."

While Jenny gathered up her notes and recorder, Sam watched Tyrone walk out of the cafeteria. She realized that had she not known about his accident, she wouldn't have noticed any difference in him at all. He really was like anybody else. Why had she always thought of him as being different?

"Ready to go?" Jen nudged her out of her thoughts.

"Uh, yeah." Samantha was still processing what she'd just heard.

"So who's next, and when do we do the interview?" Jenny was ready to move on; none of this was new to her.

Samantha had to think for a minute. "Oh, yeah, my mom was able to talk to her friend, and her friend made some phone calls. There's a girl named Allison who's getting tutoring at a rehab center. I think she broke her neck in a diving accident. Anyway, my mom's friend talked to Allison's parents, and they talked to Allison, and everybody's cool with doing an interview. I think we're on for after school on Thursday."

"Great, that will give me time to make some sense of my notes and write up Tyrone's part of the article."

"We'd better get going, don't you think? Your mom said she'd pick us up outside at 4:30 P.M. It's already 4:40 P.M. I don't want her to be mad if we're late."

"Mom won't care. She's used to me taking longer sometimes. Here, you carry, and I'll roll." Jenny grinned at Samantha as she thrust her notes and tape recorder at her. The two were fast becoming partners.

Neither realized how much they would need each other for their next interview.

Make Connections: The Difference Between Amputation and Limb Differences

Amputees are people who have had a limb surgically removed because of illness or injury.

People with limb differences are born with misshapen limbs, partial limbs, or with a limb missing.

HOW MANY PEOPLE ARE AMPUTEES?

- Amputee support organizations estimate that over three million people in the United States were born with a limb missing or lost a limb through amputation.
- Statistically, more than 50 percent of amputees have one leg amputated above the knee.
- Less than 10 percent of amputations involve the arms or hands.
- Injuries requiring amputation are twice as likely to occur in farming accidents as in any other industry.

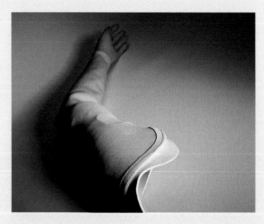

A person who has had an arm amputated may use a prosthetic arm.

A special kind of hook allows a person with an amputated hand to pick up objects.

SOME ABBREVIATIONS USED IN THE AMPUTEE COMMUNITY

Arms

- AE: Above the elbow amputation
- LAE: Above the elbow amputation of the left arm
- RAE: Above the elbow amputation of the right arm
- DAE: Double above the elbow amputation (both arms)
- BE: Below the elbow amputation
- LBE: Below the elbow amputation of the left arm
- RBE: Below the elbow amputation of the right arm
- DBE: Double below the elbow amputation (both arms)

Legs

- BK: Below the knee amputation
- LBK: Below the knee amputation of the left leg
- RBK: Below the knee amputation of the right leg
- DBK: Double below the knee amputation (both legs)
- AK: Above the knee amputation
- LAK: Above the knee amputation of the left leg
- RAK: Above the knee amputation of the right leg
- DAE: Double above the knee amputation (both legs)

COMMON CAUSES OF AMPUTATION

- disease or tumors (cancer, diabetes, leprosy, etc.)
- frostbite
- gangrene (a severe infection that kills skin and muscle tissue)
- other infections
- severe burns
- prolonged lack of blood flow to the limb
- crushing injuries (where the limb is crushed causing internal damage)
- traumatic amputation (when the limb is severed in an accident or explosion)
- entanglement injuries (when the limb is mangled or shredded after being caught in machinery or other equipment with moving parts)

WHAT TO EXPECT FROM AMPUTATION SURGERY

Surgical amputations can occur as emergency surgery in the field (like when a limb is trapped beneath the wreckage of a collapsed building) or, more commonly, in an operating room. General anesthesia, which puts a person into a deep

Some physical disabilities are congenital, the result of genetic problems present at birth.

sleep during which he cannot feel pain, is commonly used for larger limb amputations. When removing fingers or toes, local anesthesia may be used. Doctors try to save as much of the injured limb as possible, only taking what is necessary to treat the injury.

After the limb is removed, doctors cover the amputation site with a remaining flap of excess skin and sew the skin closed with special thread. They cover the remaining end of the limb with a bandage. Once the incision has completely healed and any swelling has gone down, the patient may be fitted with a prosthesis (artificial limb). Sometimes a patient may decide he would rather not use a prosthesis. In either case, physical and occupational therapy can help patients regain mobility and function.

Students with physical disabilities enjoy learning martial arts at Camp Abilities in upstate New York.

Consequences of Limb Loss

Limb loss can affect physical balance, reaction times, coordination, and overall health. It can strain remaining limbs and
muscles as they learn to compensate for the loss. Amputation can leave the patient with varying degrees of phantom
pain, a condition in which a person feels pain, itching, or
tingling in the place where the limb used to be. Phantom
pain can range from mildly annoying to completely debilitat-
ing. In addition to these physical consequences, an amputee
can also experience other losses:

- loss of the old way of doing things
- loss of a familiar body image
- loss of self-confidence
- some loss of previous activities (depending on degree
  of injury)
- sometimes job loss (depending on the nature of the
  job and of the injury)

In the face of these losses, it's important for an amputee
to realize he is not alone, that he can learn new ways of doing things, and that most amputees can do what non-am-
putees do, just in their own way.

COMMON SPORTS FOR AMPUTEES

aviation	basketball
cycling	golf
in-line skating	powered chuting
rappelling and	sailing
mountain climbing	scuba diving
skiing	soccer
track and field	weight lifting
windsurfing	

TWO AMAZING AMPUTEES

Todd Huston

When he was fourteen years old, Todd Huston got his legs tangled in a boat propeller. Because of complications that developed from his injuries, one leg had to be amputated. Several years later, after completing his education and becoming a psychotherapist, Todd, who loved mountain climbing, decided to attempt what seemed to be impossible—climb the highest elevations in every state in the United States. In 1994, Todd Huston embarked on what was called "Summit America," and he did what he set out to do. He climbed the highest summits of all fifty states in only sixty-seven days! He beat the previous record by an astounding thirty-five days. All with only one leg.

Camp Abilities allows a child with a physical disability to enjoy the thrill of participating in sports.

Research Project

Learn more about Todd Huston by going to his website: http://www.toddhuston.com. What else he accomplished? What is he doing today?

Tom Whittaker

Shortly after graduating from Idaho State University, Tom Whittaker's legs were shattered in an automobile accident. His right foot had to be amputated. The accident occurred on Thanksgiving day in 1979. Nineteen years later, on May 27, 1998, he became the first person with a physical disability to climb to the summit of Mount Everest. What's his next challenge? Tom is currently working toward becoming the first amputee to successfully climb the highest elevations in each of the seven continents.

Text-Dependent Questions

1. Which part of the body is amputated most often?
2. Explain why an amputee will lose more than just an arm or leg. What are some of the other losses he might feel?

It is when things go harder, when life becomes most trying, that there is greatest need for having a fixed goal.
—B. C. Forbes

Words to Understand

spinal cord injury (SCI): Damage done to the spinal cord through an accident or injury.

incomplete quadriplegic: Someone whose arms, legs, and trunk are paralyzed, but who retains some sensation and some ability to move in the affected limbs.

compensatory strategies: Alternate ways of accomplishing a task.

adaptive equipment: Ordinary devices that have been altered to accommodate people with physical disabilities; equipment that can alter ordinary devices to make them useable by people with disabilities.

5

TRAUMATIC SPINAL CORD INJURY: AN INTERVIEW WITH ALLISON

The first thing the two teenagers noticed when they entered the rehab center was the smell: the awful sterile smell of a hospital mixed with the smell of cafeteria food and bathroom cleaners. A rehab volunteer escorted the girls through several wide corridors complete with sloping inclines and waist-high railings along each wall. The ramps and wide halls made it easy for Jenny to navigate in her wheelchair. Her legs had been unusually tight and sore, so she opted to roll rather than try to walk with her crutches. She wanted to be undistracted for the interview.

The facility where they would meet their next interview subject was a bright, airy place with lots of windows, pastel wallpapers, and framed artwork hanging in the hallways. The assortment of watercolors, pencil drawings, and oil paintings displayed there had been done by residents of the rehab center. The artwork looked professionally framed and matted. It was very well done.

"This way." The volunteer smiled and gestured toward a final corridor. "Allison has physical therapy right now, so she thought this would be a good time for you to interview her."

The girls followed their escort into a large room about the size of half a basketball court. It looked like a gym, but with padded mats on parts of the floor, mats on top of square coffee tables, and assorted therapy devices scattered throughout the room. Jenny noted equipment with which she was familiar: pulley weights on the walls; free weights and Nautilus machines; oversize therapy balls;

parallel bars; and assorted braces, crutches, canes, walkers, and wheelchairs. She also noticed a small room off of the gym that resembled a real bedroom complete with double bed, nightstands, lamps, chairs, and a bathroom. She knew patients used this room for practicing skills they used every day but didn't think twice about until they got hurt: getting in and out of bed; turning lights on and off; maneuvering a wheelchair into the bathroom; getting in and out of a shower or tub. Yes, she'd seen much of this before in her own rehab. She felt at home.

Samantha, however, felt like an alien in a world unlike any she'd known. Rather than the equipment, her gaze focused on the people. Several people in the room not only looked different but they did strange things. Samantha noticed one middle-aged man standing at a table scrunching a towel with his hands. She saw an older woman, whose arm and face drooped like a rag doll's, walking unsteadily between the parallel bars with attendants by her sides.

Samantha saw a young girl, too, who seemed to be about six or seven years old. She wore a padded helmet, like Samantha had seen in boxing matches on TV, and sat on a purple ball almost as big as the girl. A twenty-something woman held the girl's thighs, just above her knees, and pushed her back and forth while the ball rolled beneath her. The little girl had to keep shifting her weight to keep her balance. Her arms jerked unnaturally, but Samantha couldn't tell why.

"Allison's over there." Their escort gestured toward a wheelchair stationed next to a tall, flat-top table.

Samantha and Jenny looked at each other. What they saw took them both by surprise.

Allison looked about sixteen or seventeen years old. She sat in a wheelchair unlike anything Samantha had seen Jenny use. It had a much higher back, padded side supports, and armrests. And it tilted back a bit, too. But the wheelchair didn't intimidate the girls as much as the awful metal thing attached to the teenager's head.

Allison's pretty face looked out from beneath a circle of stainless steel that surrounded her head. Four rods that looked like they went into her skull secured the metal ring to her head. Four more metal bars—two in front, two in back—held the metal ring in place by connecting it to a molded plastic harness that went over her shoulders. The harness covered the teenager's chest and shoulder blades and was held in place by padded straps that ran along her sides.

Allison's delicate voice broke the stunned silence. "It's a 'halo,' but I call it my crown. It holds my neck still while it heals. Oh, and I'm Allison, by the way. I'd offer to shake hands, but I can't use them."

Samantha and Jenny glanced down at the two braced arms resting on the wheelchair's padded armrests. The plastic splints seemed to hold Allison's hands and lower arms in what looked like a natural, relaxed position.

"Oh, ah . . . I'm sorry." Jenny was the first to recover. "I'm Jenny, and this is my friend Sam. Um, we're here to do the interview for *Yo, Girl!* magazine."

Samantha had never seen Jenny stammer for words before.

"My tutor told me about you. I'm glad I can help." It seemed so surreal: this pleasant teen voice coming out of a sci-fi looking contraption.

"Well, let's get started then. Is it okay if we tape you?" In her nervousness, Jenny dropped the tape recorder on the floor. The batteries popped out, but no damage was done. Samantha scrambled to put everything back together and then put the mini cassette machine on the high table by the wheelchair. She and Jenny exchanged glances.

"Sure. It's fine. Whatever you need to do." Allison talked deliberately while keeping her head perfectly still. She sounded weak but friendly.

The three girls began their dialogue. Samantha and Jenny learned that Allison had been a diver on her high school's diving team. Several months ago, while at a meet at an unfamiliar school, Allison dove into what she thought was a deeper section of the pool—and nailed her head on the pool bottom. Instantly she couldn't move her arms or legs. Had it not been for her coach's quick thinking when he saw his star diver lying still on the pool bottom, Allison would have drowned. He jumped in and carefully pulled the high school junior to the surface, but she'd already sustained a traumatic **spinal cord injury (SCI)**. She had fractured the C-6 vertebra in her neck.

Allison explained that C-6 referred to the location of her injury. "C" stood for the cervical section of the spine and "6" identified which vertebra in that section was injured. A person with a spinal column injury loses complete or incomplete function on both sides of the body at or below the injury site. Allison's C-6 injury meant she lost function in the parts of her body controlled by nerves found in the cervical spine's sixth vertebra and below. Her head, neck, shoulders, arms, and wrists still functioned, but she couldn't use her hands, body, legs, and feet.

After a few more questions, Jenny's nervousness ceased and she fell into her usual interview rhythm. Allison's answers differed from Tyrone's.

"What do you miss most?" Jenny asked as she wrapped up the interview.

"Two things," Allison answered. She was getting tired, the girls could tell. They waited until she completed her thought.

"People treating me normally." Allison said finally and sighed, her eyes glancing away. "I mean, like you guys, when you first saw me. I'm just a real kid with real feelings underneath all this stuff, just like you or anybody else. A lot of people can't get beyond that. Even my friends and family don't treat me the same anymore."

Samantha and Jenny looked at each other. But Jenny pressed on. "And the other thing?"

"Being independent. I mean, I'd just gotten my driver's license before I broke my neck. I really enjoyed being more on my own. Now I'm dependent on people to do *everything*. They say I'll learn to do some things for myself in time, especially since I'm an **incomplete quadriplegic**. But I'll always need help to live."

"So what do you see yourself doing when you get out of here, I mean once your neck heals and all?" It sounded like an unrealistically optimistic question to Samantha, but maybe Jen knew what she was doing.

"I want to be a writer," Allison answered quietly. The lightness of her tone faded with fatigue. "That's why I wanted to talk to you. My therapists said they could teach me to use voice dictation software so I can use a computer. Or a head stick if that doesn't work. But I know I can do that, and will someday. Do you think you could come back sometime to visit, and we could talk about writing?"

"Ah, well, sure," Jenny said. "Let's plan on it."

As they were wrapping up their dialogue, the aide returned. "That's about all the time Allison can give you right now. She gets pretty tired. Isn't that right, dear?" The aide's voice was louder as she addressed Allison and wheeled her away.

Jenny and Samantha winced. They were beginning to understand what Allison meant about people not treating her normally. Allison wasn't deaf, hard of hearing, or stupid. She had a SCI. Yet, the aide, who should have known better, treated Allison as though she had impaired hearing and was slightly mentally challenged.

Jenny let out a big sigh. "Wow. That was different than I expected. I'm glad you were here to help. I wonder what the next one's going to be like."

STATISTICS ABOUT SPINAL CORD INJURIES

The University of Alabama at Birmingham's National Spinal Cord Injury Statistical Center cites these interesting facts:

- About 7,800 new SCIs occur each year in the United States (low estimate).
- Between 250,000 and 400,000 people live with SCI or spinal dysfunction today.
- Motor vehicle accidents are the leading cause of SCI, accounting for 44 percent of SCIs.
- Acts of violence are the second leading cause of SCI, accounting for 24 percent.
- After the age of forty-five, falls become the leading cause of SCI.
- Sports injuries account for only eight percent of SCIs.
- Two-thirds of all sport-related SCIs come from diving.
- Males account for 82 percent of all people with SCIs.
- SCIs happen most often between the ages of sixteen and thirty.

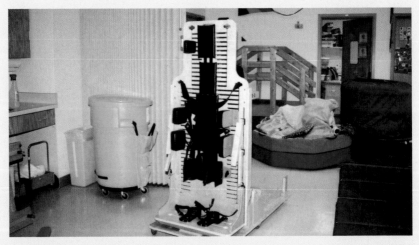

Physical therapy involves many activities and equipment.

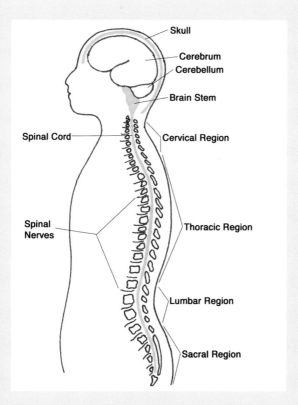

- The most frequent age of injury is nineteen years old.
- The fastest growing cause of SCI is violence.

According to the CDC, young African American males face the greatest risk of sustaining SCIs.

SPINAL CORD ANATOMY

The spinal cord is made up of four primary sections: the cervical, thoracic, lumbar, and sacral regions. How disabled a person with a SCI becomes depends on where along the spinal column his injury occurs.

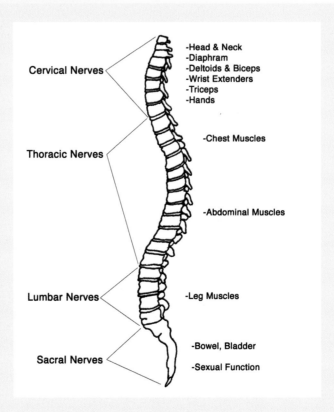

- Head & Neck
- Diaphram
- Deltoids & Biceps
- Wrist Extenders
- Triceps
- Hands

- Chest Muscles

- Abdominal Muscles

- Leg Muscles

- Bowel, Bladder

- Sexual Function

Cervical Nerves

Thoracic Nerves

Lumbar Nerves

Sacral Nerves

Spinal Cord Functions by Region

Each part of the spine is identified with a letter and a number. The letter stands for the region: C = cervical; T = thoracic; L = lumbar; and S = sacral. The number identifies the vertebrae within that region: 1 = highest, all succeeding numbers count down the spine (2 under 1, 3 under 2, etc.) from top to bottom. A person with a T-12 SCI would have sustained their injury at the twelfth vertebra in the thoracic region. A person with a SCI loses function at their level of injury and below. Our person with a T-12 SCI, then, would not have full use of his legs, bowel, bladder, or sexual function.

WHAT CAN OCCUPATIONAL AND PHYSICAL THERAPISTS DO FOR A PERSON WITH SCI?

Physical and occupational therapists do many of the same things, but physical therapists focus on the larger muscles. The American Occupational Therapy Association affirms that occupational therapists can help SCI patients by doing the following:

1. Evaluating how much function and ability the patient still has after the injury, not just in the hospital but at home, at work, and while participating in recreational activities.
2. Determining how much the patient wants to participate in pre-injury activities.
3. Providing one-on-one retraining in ADL (bathing, dressing, grooming, feeding, cooking, writing, using appliances, etc.) by teaching **compensatory strategies** and providing instruction on the use of **adaptive equipment** where necessary.
4. Determining what kinds of ATDs would help the patient the most and allow him to reach the greatest level of independence.
5. Facilitating ways to overcome lasting effects of SCI, not just by providing adaptive equipment and compensatory strategies but by teaching coping skills as well.
6. Designing and implementing exercise regimens that strengthen muscles used in everyday living and help maintain the patient's overall fitness.
7. Identifying how the roles of a person with a SCI have to change and providing strategies to help him transition from pre-injury roles to realistic post-injury ones.

Special equipment allows individuals to learn to cope with spinal injuries.

COPING WITH A SPINAL CORD INJURY

1. Allow yourself to grieve the "loss" of the old you.
2. Accept that anger, sadness, denial, frustration, jealousy, loneliness, and other emotions are a normal part of the recovery process. Allow them to steer you toward acceptance.
3. Get involved in your treatment plan. Participate in team meetings. Talk to doctors.
4. Educate yourself about your injury and its consequences.
5. Set goals, no matter how small, and work toward them.
6. Focus on what you can do, and work toward improving those abilities.

7. Realize that a full, meaningful life is possible after SCI; it just may be a different life.
8. Be open to trying new things or to developing new interests.
9. Try not to think in all-or-nothing terms: always or never; everyone or no one. Rather, think accurately: *Some* things may not be possible, but some are; *some* injuries are permanent, but some improve, etc.
10. Expect occasional setbacks, but don't let them defeat you.

HOW TO PREVENT SPINAL CORD INJURIES

The CDC, the Spinal Cord Injury Information Network, and other organizations suggest these tips to prevent spinal cord injuries:

- Always wear a seat belt, whether driving or riding in a car.
- Wear a helmet when riding a horse, bike, motorcycle, or other motorized vehicles.
- During sports, wear *all* required safety gear.
- When playing baseball, never slide head first into a base.
- In gymnastics, always use a spotter.
- When swimming, always check the water's depth before diving in.
- Never dive into unknown or murky waters. Never dive into shallow waters.
- Follow instructions and safety procedures when using power equipment.
- Use hand railings on stairways.
- Don't take unnecessary risks while engaging in dangerous sports (snow or water skiing, rock

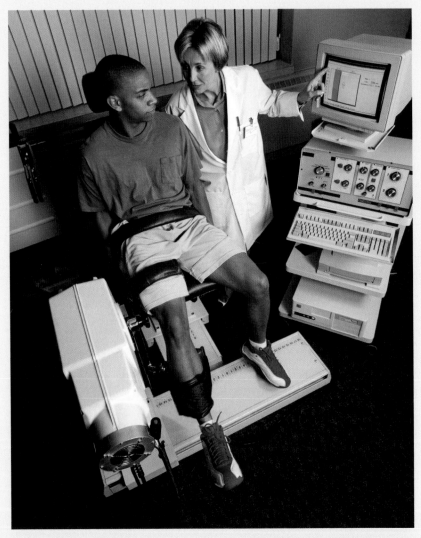

Various technologies play a role in helping individuals cope with physical injuries.

Research Project

Go online to find out more about occupational and physical therapists. How much education does each of these jobs require? What personal strengths would you need to do these jobs? What do you think is most rewarding about these jobs? What do you think is hardest? Are either of these careers you would consider for yourself? Why or why not?

climbing, hang gliding, snowboarding, horseback riding and jumping, etc.).

- Never jump on a trampoline with another person. Only one person should jump at a time.
- Never drink alcohol or take drugs while participating in high-risk activities.
- Never drink alcohol or take drugs before operating power equipment or driving a car.
- Never ride with someone who has been drinking or taking drugs.

Text-Dependent Questions

1. What causes most spinal cord injuries?
2. How old are most people when their spinal cords are injured?
3. Describe some of the ways occupational and physical therapists can help people with spinal cord injury.
4. List some ways you can prevent a spinal cord injury from happening to you.

When it comes right down to it, there is no "them."
There is only "us."
—Katherine Mill

Words to Understand

birth defect: A physical abnormality that is present at birth.
Duchenne muscular dystrophy (DMD): The most severe form of muscular dystrophy.
progressive: A condition that gets worse with time.
seizures: Sudden episodes where the central nervous system's electrical rhythms are disturbed, clouding consciousness.
scoliosis: A condition where the spinal column bends or curves inappropriately.
shunt: A special tube inserted into the body to drain excess fluid.

6

Spina Bifida:
An Interview with Katie

Compared to Allison's interview at the rehab center, the interview scheduled with Katie Miles should have been a piece of cake. Katie was a fifteen-year-old who'd had spina bifida since birth. Spina bifida, the girls learned in their pre-interview research, is a **birth defect** that happens when the protective covering that surrounds a developing baby's spinal cord doesn't close completely while the infant is in its mother's womb. These babies are born with an opening in their spines that allows damage to be done to the spinal cord. The opening can occur anywhere along the spine, but the higher the opening, the more disabled the person will be. Katie's opening had been low on her spine, so only the lower part of her body and legs were affected.

Katie lived at home with her parents in a comfortable, single-story house, much like anyone else's. She used special crutches or a walker to get around. Katie attended school in a neighboring school district, rode a regular bus, and was an honors student taking advanced classes. What Jenny and Samantha thought would be routine, however, turned out to be a lesson in the realities of life with paralysis—bodily functions and all.

"Yuck! You mean you really have to check yourself throughout the day?" Samantha blurted out in the middle of the interview when Katie honestly answered Jen's question about how her paralysis impacted her everyday life. The fifteen-year-old explained that since she couldn't feel the need to go to the bathroom the way people without paralysis do, she had to check her underwear and special pads she wore several times a day to see if she was starting to go.

"It's just one of the tricks they taught us at a bowel management workshop I attended. They're 'tricks of the trade' that help people with spina bifida become more independent and avoid embarrassing situations. I mean, having to go to the bathroom isn't something to be ashamed of; it's how all of our bodies work, paralysis or no paralysis. It's just that people with spina bifida or other spinal injuries have to handle it differently."

Samantha again was amazed at the grace and ease with which Katie talked about private things. Everyone she and Jen had interviewed so far seemed comfortable talking about their situations, no matter how involved their disabilities were.

"So what happens if you have an accident?" Jen followed up without flinching.

"I always carry a 'clean-up kit' with me. That means a washcloth, soap, small towel, plastic bag for dirty clothing, clean undies, a mirror to make sure I'm clean, and a change of my special pads. I keep my kit in my backpack; most people don't even know it's there."

Katie's matter-of-factness astounded Samantha. It seemed like people with disabilities could talk about *anything* without embarrassment. In a weird sort of way, Samantha envied the camaraderie Jen shared with her disabled peers. It seemed like they had their own little club, a club to which the able-bodied could not belong.

"Well, how does something like that affect your ability to participate in everyday things, like school, or field trips, or concert rehearsals and competitions?" Jen had learned that Katie was part of the competitive concert choir. Apparently she'd made regional chorus that year.

"When I was younger, I was scared to get involved in things. I was always afraid of having an accident or of smelling bad or of other people finding out that I wore special pads. Now, it's more like it's just a fact of life. And if I handle things with honesty and a sense of humor, then other people seem to accept me as I am. I mean it's good to learn to laugh at ourselves now and then, right? It also helps that my closest friends know—they help me if I need them to. But I don't tell everyone. That would just be stupid. Not *everybody* needs to know all the details."

Jen nodded in understanding. "You can say that again."

Samantha again sensed an unspoken understanding between these two teens with very different challenges. Samantha was surprised by the jealousy she sensed creeping up on her again.

Jenny wrapped up their interview with Katie, and then she and Sam got back into the car. Mrs. Vanderhoff had driven the girls to Katie's home and had talked with Katie's mom during the interview. Now they settled in for the hour-long ride home.

"Can I ask you something, Jen?" Samantha began cautiously.

"Sure. Anything wrong? You seem quiet."

"Not really. Um . . . well, I guess. I don't know how to ask you this." Samantha searched for a way to say what she wanted to say.

"Ask me what? Just blurt it out."

Samantha softened her voice to a near whisper. She didn't want Mrs. Vanderhoff to hear. "How come you seem so comfortable with the kids we're interviewing? I mean, you don't know them, yet you fit right in. Even with Allison, once you got started. Me, on the other hand, I'm grossed out or weirded out or uncomfortable. It's like I don't know how to connect with them."

"That's just it, Sam. You answered your own question."

"What do you mean? I didn't answer anything."

"Sure you did. You said you don't know how to connect with *them*. That's just it. I don't see kids with challenges as *them*. I see *them* as *us*. We're people. Period. We may look different on the outside, or do things differently, but we're all just kids with hopes and dreams and feelings and disappointments. *Every* teen, able-bodied and challenged alike, has those things. When I see an Allison or a Tyrone, or a Katie, they're just kids to me. Just like me inside. But I guess I wouldn't know that if it weren't for these." Jenny gestured to her legs.

"How can I learn to see kids with challenges that way? I mean like you do. I don't have physical challenges."

Jenny didn't seem bothered by Samantha's honesty. "Focus on the person inside the body, not on the body itself. Focus on who they are, not on what they can or cannot do. If that's too hard, try focusing on their abilities, not on their disabilities. Just get to know them. You'll see. You'll start to feel more comfortable in no time. I mean, you're comfortable around me, right?"

"Yeah, well that's different. I mean you're normal."

Jenny laughed out loud. "Yeah, right. And I can run hurdles, too."

Both girls laughed.

Their humor, however, wouldn't be enough to get them through the remaining interview on their list. The last interview was scheduled to be with a sixteen-year-old guy named Ben who had **_Duchenne muscular dystrophy (DMD)_**. Unlike the other teens, he had a **_progressive_** disease, not just a permanent physical challenge. The disease would get worse, and there was nothing funny about that.

FACTS ABOUT SPINA BIFIDA

The CDC's National Center for Health Statistics estimates that 20 out of every 100,000 babies born in the United States have spina bifida. That's 1 out of every 5,000 births.

The Mayo Clinic's numbers run higher, estimating that spina bifida affects 1,500 to 2,000 babies born in the United States each year, or 1 out of every 2,000 live births.

The Spina Bifida Association (SBA) paints an even darker picture: Their statistics indicate that spina bifida affects 1 out of every 1,000 live births per year. The SBA also estimates that spina bifida and a related condition called anencephaly affect 4,000 pregnancies per year in the United States, or roughly eleven pregnancies per day.

Spina bifida is the most common birth defect resulting in permanent disabilities. Seventy to 90 percent of those born with the severest form of spina bifida also have trouble with too much fluid collecting in their brains, a condition call hydrocephalus ("hydro" refers to water; "cephalus" refers to brain). About one in twenty people with spina bifida also experiences **seizures**.

NEURAL TUBE DEFECTS

Doctors classify spina bifida as a neural tube defect (NTD). The neural tube is made up of the brain, the spinal cord, and their protective membranes. When any of these structures fails to develop properly, it is called a neural tube defect. There are three types of NTDs:

- Anencephaly: when a baby's brain never develops or is underdeveloped. These babies do not usually survive more than a few hours after they are born.
- Encephalocele: when a baby's skull doesn't close completely and the resulting hole allows brain tissue

Make Connections: The Spine

Several bones called vertebrae stack together to form the spine (or spinal column). Each vertebra has a hole in the center that, combined with the other vertebrae, creates a long vertical tunnel in the spine through which passes the nerve highway that carries messages between the brain and various body parts. This nerve highway, made up of nerve tissue and its protective membrane, the meninges, is called the spinal cord. The spinal cord runs inside the spinal column. Cushioning pads, called discs, rest between each of the vertebra that makes up the spinal column. These work like shock absorbers to protect the spine and spinal cord from injury.

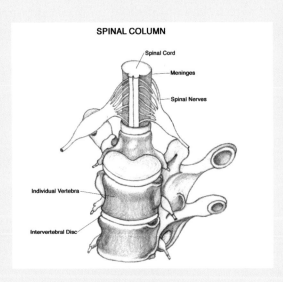

to protrude. These babies rarely survive. If they do, they have severe intellectual disabilities.
- Spina bifida: when part of the spinal column doesn't close completely and the spinal cord or its protective coverings poke through the hole. "Spina" means "spine" and "bifida" means "split in two" or "open."

TYPES OF SPINA BIFIDA

The National Information Center for Children and Youth with Disabilities (NICHCY) identifies three types of spina bifida:

- Spina bifida occulta: This is a "hidden" condition in which one or more vertebrae in the spinal column fail to close completely, but no damage is done to the spinal cord. Between 20 and 40 percent of all Americans have this condition, but because it results in no permanent disability and has few symptoms, most people don't even know they have it.
- Meningocele: This is a repairable condition that happens when the meninges, the protective covering surrounding the spinal cord, pushes through an opening in the bones of the spine creating a sac called a meningocele. The spinal cord itself is not damaged, and surgery can correct the condition without causing long-term disability.
- Myelomeningocele: This form of spina bifida is responsible for most spina bifida-related disabilities and is usually what people think of when they say "spina bifida." In this form, the spinal cord itself pushes through an opening in the spinal column, causing irreparable damage to the nerves in the spinal cord.

Like many other children, kids with physical disabilities enjoy opportunities to play sports.

The room where children receive physical therapy is often a bright, cheerful place with plenty of fascinating and fun equipment to help young patients cope with their disabilities.

SPINA BIFIDA AND PHYSICAL CHALLENGES

Because spina bifida damages the spinal cord, people with this condition experience many of the same disabilities as do people with traumatic spinal cord injuries. Some common effects of spina bifida include:

- Complete or partial paralysis at the damage site and below.
- The need for mobility aids (wheelchairs, crutches, walkers, etc.).

Research Project

Use the Internet to find out what spina bi-fida researchers are working on. Describe some of the studies they're doing. How could their work help people with spina bifida?

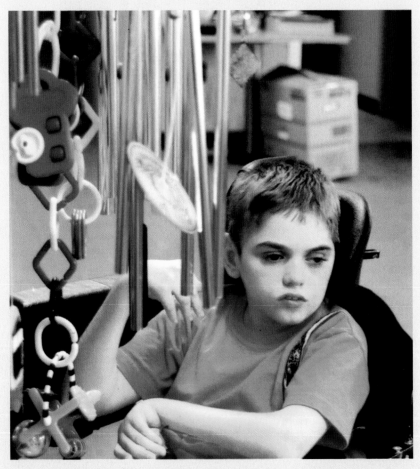

This sixteen-year-old boy looks much younger. Physical disabilities can often interfere with normal growth patterns.

Text-Dependent Questions

1. Why do people with spina bifida have many of the same challenges as people with spinal cord injuries?
2. What kind of spina bifida could a person have without ever knowing?
3. How has life changed for people with spina bifida in the past sixty years?

- Problems with bowel and bladder management.
- **Scoliosis** (curved backbone).
- Osteoporosis (thinning of the bones) in unused limbs.
- Some degree of sexual dysfunction.
- Hydrocephalus (excess fluid collection in the brain).
- The need for a **shunt** to be implanted in the brain to drain the excess fluid into another part of the body where it can be absorbed without causing damage.
- Seizures.

THEN AND NOW

As recently as the 1950s, most children born with spina bifida died. Today, thanks to advances in surgical treatment of this disorder (both in the womb and out) and because of better infection control, many people with this condition grow up to graduate from high school, go to college, get married, and have successful careers. Some are even able to have children. With hard work and determination, people with spina bifida can lead rich, meaningful lives.

My dream is to make peace
throughout the world with my books.
—Mattie Stepanek, 13-year-old with muscular dystrophy

Words to Understand

genetic: Passed from one generation to the next through a person's genes.

ventilators: Machines that help a person breathe.

tracheotomy: A medical procedure in which a tube is inserted into the airway at the base of a person's neck.

7

MUSCULAR DYSTROPHY: AN INTERVIEW WITH BEN

"I think the thing I've learned the most from having DMD is that it's all about attitude. Life's only about one-tenth of what you're dealt; the other nine-tenths is what you do with what you're dealt. I mean, I can't control what hand I'm given, but I can control how I react to that hand."

Ben sat slightly bent over in his high-back wheelchair, a wide strap, like a seat belt, pulled snugly around his chest. Like the other teens interviewed, Ben was matter-of-fact when talking about his challenges. Diagnosed when he was six years old, he started using a wheelchair part time by age ten. When he reached his early teens, Ben became completely wheelchair dependent. Now he uses a motorized wheelchair because his arms are no longer strong enough to propel him.

Samantha and Jenny knew from the preparation they'd done for this interview that Duchenne muscular dystrophy was the most severe form of muscular dystrophy (MD). All types of MD are *genetic*, and all types involve increasing muscle weakness and a sickening of the muscles that control movement. In Duchenne's, however, symptoms show up earlier, often during preschool years, and progress much faster. Kids diagnosed with DMD usually live only until their late teens or early twenties. Only boys get Duchenne's, and it is always fatal. Death usually occurs from lung or heart failure caused by degeneration of the heart or respiratory muscles or from infections.

"I'm one of the lucky ones," Ben continued.

Lucky? Samantha thought. *How can he see himself as lucky? Ten years ago he was a lot like other kids his age. Now he can't even push his own wheelchair. Lucky?*

"Most of my MD friends, the ones who are my age, are on vents by now," Ben continued, "which means they have trachs, too."

"What are vents and trachs?" Jenny asked, professional as ever.

"**Ventilators** and **tracheotomy** tubes. A ventilator is a machine that breathes for you, and a trach tube is how the machine is attached. Doctors do an operation to insert a tube into your trachea," Ben explained, gesturing clumsily to the front part of the base of his neck. "Then they attach the tube to a hose that's attached to the ventilator, which pumps oxygenated air into your lungs and pulls the used air out. People with MD whose chest muscles get weak enough eventually need a vent. It's just part of the disease."

"So you think you'll need to go on a vent sometime?" Jenny again plowed ahead.

"I *know* I will. It's just a matter of time. It's either that or die, I suppose."

For once, Jenny could think of nothing to say. How do you talk about dying with a sixteen-year-old?

Ben sensed the girls' awkwardness.

"Don't be afraid to talk about dying," he said. "We're all going to die someday, sooner or later. You, too. It's just that some of us go earlier than others. When you live with a disease that you know is going to kill you, you start to realize that death is part of life—for all of us. You learn to make the most of the time you've got."

Samantha and Jenny still didn't know what to say. So Ben continued. "Look. I know there's no cure for DMD. All doctors can do is treat my symptoms. They do everything they can for all the colds I get, and I get plenty. I've had pneumonia twice already. And they do what they can for the curve in my spine, which is what makes me look all bent over like this."

Ben looked out from under his tilted head and grinned at the now-silent interviewers. "You were wondering about that, weren't you? Most people do. It's called scoliosis, and it's just part of having DMD." He paused to take a breath. "But anything doctors do is a Band-Aid; they can't cure me. But you know what? You learn to take it as it comes. And you learn to be thankful for little things."

"Like what?" Jen had found her voice again, but Samantha still sat there taking it all in.

"Like that I'm not in pain. That's the funny thing about DMD. It's not really painful. It'll kill you, and it will rob you of your ability to move and breathe on your own, but it won't put you in agonizing pain. That's a huge thing—in my book anyway."

Ben stopped to think for a moment. "Oh, and it makes me thankful for things like the sweetness of a milkshake going down my throat or the feeling of a breeze on my face. Simple pleasures most people don't even notice—I'm learning to appreciate them. I know I only have so much time to enjoy all of it, so I try to savor it one small thing at a time.

Jen made a visible effort to get her interviewing stride back. "Do you ever get discouraged? I mean do you ever feel sad or mad or frustrated or jealous? Do you ever feel sorry for yourself?"

"Sure I do. I wouldn't be human if I didn't. But I try not to waste too much energy on all that. I just know that I can't change things, so why waste the time I have on being angry with everybody or feeling sorry for myself? There are so many things I can still do, so many people to enjoy, so many friends I haven't met yet."

Friends I haven't met yet. Where have I heard that before? Samantha's thoughts swirled through her mind.

"The world could learn a lot from you, Ben," she said quietly. Apart from introducing herself at the start of the interview, it was the only thing she'd said during their entire time together. She was trying to process everything he said.

Ben's words reminded her of BJ Twiam's reply to the letter she'd sent what seemed like forever ago. BJ's attitude then reflected Ben's now: yes, grieve your losses, but be alert for the countless good things you have or what may be waiting for you just around the corner.

Samantha reflected on how angry she'd been about Ali's move, how sorry she'd felt for herself about the relocation of a friend, and how blind she was to the possibility of new friendships. Compared to the continual losses Ben faced every day, her losses seemed so small. No one, she realized, was saying she couldn't be sad; she should be. It was okay to grieve. But what Samantha saw in Ben and Jenny and all the others they'd interviewed was an attitude that said, "Yeah, life's hard sometimes, and sometimes it's downright nasty, but don't let the bad stuff blind you to the good." It was a lesson she'd carry with her always.

FACTS ON MUSCULAR DYSTROPHY

- Muscular dystrophy (MD) is not a single disorder; it is the common name for a group of disorders that cause muscles to weaken and waste away over time.
- It is generally accepted that there are nine types of muscular dystrophy, though there are additional related disorders.
- Muscular dystrophy can affect children and adults, depending on the type of MD.
- All types of muscular dystrophy are caused by abnormalities in a person's genes. MD is *not* contagious.
- There is still no way to prevent or cure muscular dystrophy.
- The most common form of MD in children is Duchenne muscular dystrophy (DMD), and it affects only boys.
- The Muscular Dystrophy Association (MDA) estimates that one in every 3,500 male live births has DMD.
- The most common form of MD in adults is myotonic muscular dystrophy, sometimes called Steinert's disease.

DUCHENNE DYSTROPHY

Typical Progression of the Disease

Birth to two years: The affected child develops like other children.

Two to six years: Symptoms appear. Pelvic and leg muscles weaken first, causing him to walk differently. He may not be able to keep up with other children, may fall frequently, and may have difficulty going up steps or getting up from a sitting position. He may walk more on his toes, and his calves may become enlarged.

Six to twelve years: The young boy's muscles continue to lose strength. Shoulder and arms start to weaken, but arm weakness doesn't progress as fast as weakness in the legs. Boys with DMD start using a wheelchair at least part time by the time they reach eight or ten years old.

After twelve years: Virtually all DMD patients use wheelchairs full time by the time they enter their teen years. At first a boy with DMD may propel his own wheelchair, but as his arms and shoulders weaken, he eventually needs a motorized wheelchair. He will lose the ability to lift his arms or to raise his hands to his mouth. He will not be able to feed or groom himself. Muscle weakness continues to advance and will eventually include his chest, heart, and lung muscles. In later stages, he will need a machine to help him breathe.

What Causes DMD?

All forms of muscular dystrophy come from a problem with a person's genetic makeup. The DNA found in a person's genes contains a "code" or set of "instructions" for making and maintaining healthy muscles. These instructions tell the body how to produce certain proteins that build and maintain muscle fiber. In a person with MD, these instructions are missing, incomplete, or mistaken. If the instructions are missing, a person will develop one type of MD; if the instructions are mistaken, a person will develop another type of MD. The specific problem with the instructions determines what kind of MD a person has.

The defective gene that causes MD may be inherited; it is

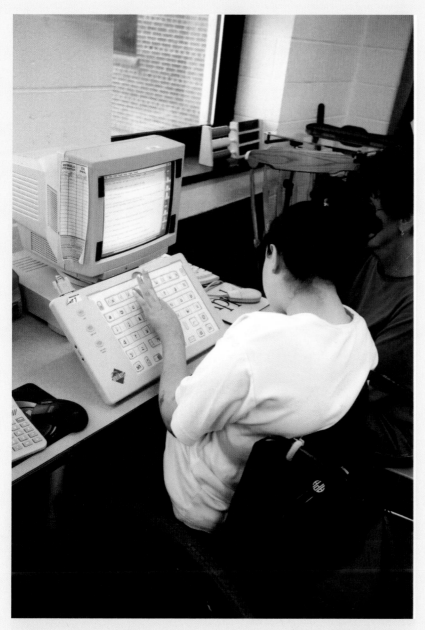

Most teens with DMD will need to use a wheelchair, both at school and at home.

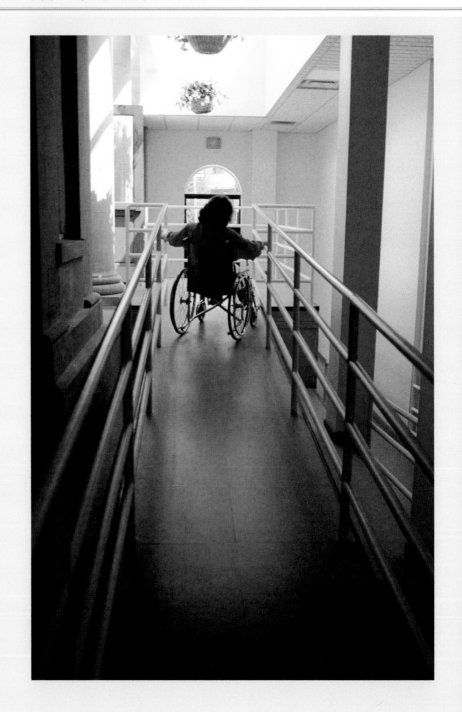

passed from a parent to the child at the moment of conception. It may also arise spontaneously in a child whose parents are neither carriers of the gene. This happens very early in the developing fetus, well before birth.

What Kinds of Equipment Does Someone with DMD Need?

As a young child, a boy with DMD doesn't need special equipment. But as his muscles weaken over time, he will need many types of equipment depending on the stage of the disease. All DMD patients can expect to eventually need the following:

- Wheelchairs: Perhaps manual at first, but ultimately motorized.
- Home modifications: Ramps, railings, grab bars in the bathroom and shower, etc.
- Adapted clothing: Velcro closures instead of buttons, open fronts instead of pullovers, elastic waists instead of snaps and zippers, slip-on shoes instead of laces, etc.
- Special mattresses or hospital beds: To reduce bed sores and discomfort when the patient can no longer roll over or sit up on his own.
- Powered lifts: In a conversion van, or for going up and down stairs.
- Ventilator: A machine that breathes for the patient when he can no longer breathe on his own.

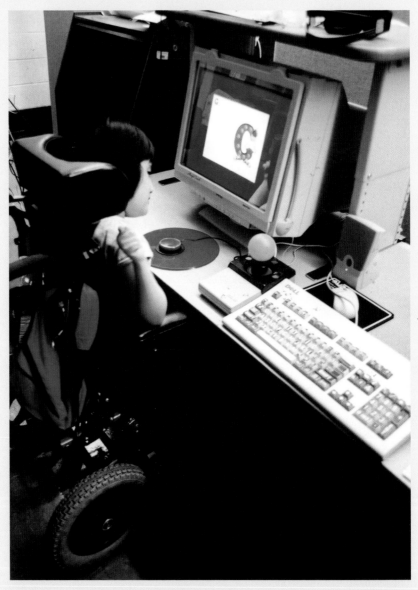

Children with DMD and other physical disabilities may attend special schools designed to meet their needs—but in many cases they will attend regular public schools, where support services give them the extra help they need.

Diagnosing DMD

In April 2003, the National Institute of Neurological Disorders and Stroke (NINDS) announced that researchers developed a new, simple, inexpensive blood test that detects DMD with a 95 percent accuracy rate. The new test is called Single Condition Amplification/Internal Primer sequencing (SCAIP), and it examines a person's genes for abnormalities that cause DMD. Females cannot be tested using SCAIP. Doctors also continue to use these older tests to diagnose DMD:

- Other blood tests: These tests measure enzyme levels. Since MD causes muscles to release more enzymes than normal, high levels of certain enzymes can indicate MD.
- Muscle biopsy: This procedure involves removing a sample of muscle tissue from the patient and examining it for the missing or deformed muscle protein that causes DMD.
- DNA testing: This involves getting DNA samples, which can be obtained by rubbing a cotton swab inside the mouth, and looking for the flawed gene.
- Electromyogram (EMG): Small wires, called electrodes, are inserted into the muscles to measure electrical activity.

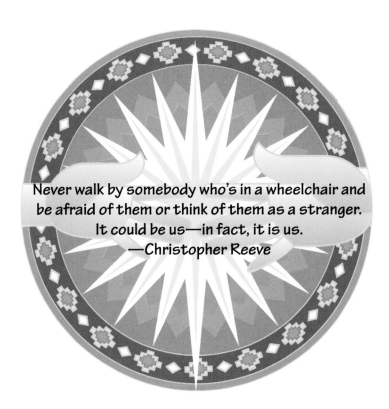

Never walk by somebody who's in a wheelchair and
be afraid of them or think of them as a stranger.
It could be us—in fact, it is us.
—Christopher Reeve

8

DISABLED, NOT UNABLE

"Sam! Yo, Sam!" Samantha heard someone calling, but the voice seemed far away. Maybe it was part of her dream, a pleasant dream from which she didn't want to wake. A cool breeze caressed her face as she lounged across the comforter that covered her four-poster bed. How good it felt to doze a while. But then she heard that voice again.

"SAM!"

This time her eyes popped open.

"SAMANTHA STEVENSON! YO!"

Jen? Why would Jenny be yelling for me at this time of day?

Samantha rolled over and looked through her open, screened window. On her neighbors' driveway below, her best friend sat in her wheelchair holding a stack of who-knows-what on her lap. She yelled again, cupping one hand like a megaphone around her mouth while waving something in the other.

"SAM! You've got to come down. It's here! Didn't I tell you? It's here!" Jenny couldn't contain the excitement in her voice. It sounded like she'd won the lottery.

Samantha bolted upright. *The article! It's here. It's really here!* "Be right down!"

She scrambled off her bed, raced downstairs, and ran out to the driveway. Jenny's lap held seven copies of the September issue of *Yo, Girl!* She held an eighth copy in her hand. Looking over Jen's shoulder Samantha watched as the first two pages of a gorgeous four-page spread opened before her. The article title read, "Disabled, Not Unable." Its subtitle was more telling: "Five Challenged Teens Who Change the World One Life at a Time." As Sam read the line beneath the subtitle, her heart skipped a beat: "by Jenny Vanderhoff and Samantha Stevenson." The best friends were now coauthors, too!

"This is way cool!" Samantha flipped through the article.

"Congratulations! You're a published writer now."

The girls high-fived each other and began reading through their own copies of the article: Jen in her wheelchair, Sam sitting in the grass beside her.

Nearly three months had gone by since they'd completed their interviews, gone through their notes and recordings, written the article, and submitted it for publication. Three months was a pretty fast turnaround, but their editors liked the article so much that they decided to run it in their September back-to-school issue.

After brief recaps of Jen's cerebral palsy, Tyrone's amputation, Allison's spinal cord injury, Katie's spina bifida, and Ben's muscular dystrophy, the article focused on how much all these individuals shared in common with other teens: Jen's love of basketball, Tyrone's joy of running, Allison's dream to be a writer someday, Katie's need to overcome her fears, and Ben's powerful lessons about attitude. The feature breathed optimism and hope in the face of overwhelming odds. It was exactly the tone both girls had hoped for.

As Jenny scanned the article's last page, though, she noticed the last interview had been changed. The original last section contained Jen's interview with Samantha, the one she requested at the start of the assignment; it was supposed to be an able-bodied teen's perspective on teens with challenges. But, unknown to Jen, Samantha contacted the editors to ask if she could make it more personal. She'd rewritten the last section to read:

Challenged Teens Do Change Lives

When my coauthor, Jenny Vanderhoff, asked me to help her with this article, I was scared at first. As an able-bodied teen, what could I possibly have in common with teens with disabilities? I mean, I didn't even want to meet Jenny when she moved in next door; she used a wheelchair, and I missed my old best friend too much. Once I met Jenny, I still didn't want to get to know her because I told her I didn't like columnist BJ Twiam's reply to a letter I wrote to this magazine. I was embarrassed when I learned that Jenny really is BJ (BJ Twiam is her pen name), and I didn't think I could face her again. I'd said some really mean things. But Jenny, a.k.a. BJ, didn't let my criticism bug her. She liked me for being "me," not for what I did or said. She accepted me, mistakes and all, and that made me want to do the article.

Working on this article has forever changed the way I look at people with challenges. Instead of seeing people who "can't," I just see people. I see teens who have the same hopes and dreams and fears and desires to be loved that anyone else has. And I see people who "can." Who can offer so much. Who can teach me. Who can change the world.

What do they teach? Each one taught me something different: Focus on ability.

Look forward and dream.

Laugh now and then, and you can handle just about anything with the right attitude.

But mostly I think I learned that life is hard sometimes for each one of us, whether we have to lose a friend or lose a leg, but I can't let that blind me to the good things that surround me every day. I almost let the loss of one friend keep me from making a new one. And that would've been a real tragedy.

Thanks Tyrone, Allison, Katie, and Ben. Thanks for teaching me that we're all the same inside and that what's on the outside really doesn't matter much. And thanks, Jen, for being my new best friend. You've started changing the world by changing me—and that's changing the world one life at a time.

Love,
Sam

Jenny finished reading and looked for Samantha. She'd been so engrossed in the changed article that she hadn't heard Samantha get up and go into the garage.

"You up for more hoops, girlfriend?" Samantha called, carrying out the basketball.

Jen held up the magazine and pointed to the last part of the article.

"Yup." Samantha grinned. "I rewrote it, and I meant every word."

"What . . . ? I mean, I don't know what to say."

"You don't have to say anything. Just put the magazines down and let's play some ball. We don't have that much time to play, you know."

"What do you mean?"

"Well, I called the rehab center we visited and they said tonight would be a good time for us to visit Allison again to coach her on her writing. In the last three months, she's learned how to use the voice-activated computer software she mentioned when we interviewed her, and she's been writing up a storm. Your mom said she could drive us. So, what d'ya say? A little hoops, then off to meet with another writer?"

"You bet I'm up for it," Jenny answered. "Anything for a friend."

DIFFERENT CHALLENGES AT A GLANCE

The five teens covered in Samantha and Jenny's article faced different physical challenges with different causes and effects in their lives.

Condition	Onset of Condition	Physical Challenges	Is it lifelong?	Does it get worse
cerebral palsy (Jenny)	usually before, at, or shortly after birth	permanent muscle weakness or tightness, poor motor control and coordination; varies in severity	yes	no
amputation (Tyrone)	can occur any time in life	loss of a limb, but other body parts usually unaffected; can impact overall health.	from point of injury on	no, but can have complications
limb differences	usually before birth	only involved limb affected; involves loss of part of a limb or deformity of affected limb	yes	not usually
traumatic spinal cord injury (Allison)	can occur at any time in life	depends on location of injury, but results in partial or complete paralysis	from point of injury on	not usually
spina bifida (Katie)	usually within the first twenty-eight days of conception	depends on location of injury, but usually results in some degree of paralysis in addition to other medical conditions	yes	no, but has complications
Duchenne muscular dystrophy (Ben)	genetic; happens at conception; symptoms appear in childhood	progressive weakening of all muscles; ultimately results in death	yes	yes

Make Connections:
Famous People with Physical Challenges

Olympic gold-medalist and former professional baseball player Jim Abbott was born with only one hand.

Canadian-born actor Michael J. Fox has Parkinson's disease, a slowly progressing disease of the nervous system.

Acclaimed violinist Itzhak Perlman lives with permanently paralyzed legs due to polio he contracted when he was four years old.

Christopher Reeve was a renowned activist, director, and actor of Superman fame who shattered his C1 and C2 vertebrae in a 1995 horseback-riding accident. He died from complications from his paralysis in 2004.

Mattie Stepanek, a teenager with muscular dystrophy, was the author of five best-selling books. He died from MD in 2004.

Bill Porter, award-winning Watkins Company salesperson and subject of the TNT movie *Door to Door*, has cerebral palsy.

Kids with physical disabilities may surprise everyone with their achievements!

The Americans with Disabilities Act provides for handicapped accessibility in public places.

LEGAL PROTECTIONS FOR PEOPLE WITH PHYSICAL DISABILITIES

Two important laws allow people with physical disabilities to reach their potentials like never before.

The Americans with Disabilities Act (ADA) of 1990

This legislation makes it illegal to discriminate against someone with disabilities in employment, in state and local government, in transportation, in public places and accommodations, and in telecommunications.

The Individuals with Disabilities Education Act (IDEA) of 1990

This federal law requires every state in the United States to provide a free, appropriate education for all children, including those with disabilities. This includes the development of an *individualized education plan (IEP)* for any child needing special education and the provision of appropriate related services (transportation, therapies, etc.). An IEP is a written plan designed specifically for each special education child. It defines reasonable expectations for achievement and how success will be determined. It should include these points:

1. A statement of the child's current level of educational performance.
2. A statement of goals or achievements expected for each area of identified weakness by the end of the school year.
3. Short-term objectives stated in instructional terms (concrete, observable steps leading to the mastery of the yearly goals).

Text-Dependent Questions

1. Why isn't muscular dystrophy contagious?
2. Describe the six kinds of equipment a person with muscular dystrophy will need.
3. Explain why IDEA is so important to people with physical challenges.

Research Project

Use the Internet or library to find out more about one of the people listed in this chapter who have or had physical challenges. Answer these questions:

- How did this person's physical challenge come about?
- How did it affect his life?
- How did he learn to cope with it?
- What has this person accomplished in life?
- How does this story compare to the stories in this book? How is it similar? How is it different?

4. A statement of the specific special education and support services to be provided to the child.
5. A statement of the extent to which a child will be able to participate in regular education programs and justification for any special placement recommended.
6. Projected dates for the beginning of services and how long they are anticipated to last.
7. A statement of the criteria and evaluation procedures to be used in determining (on at least an annual basis, if not more frequently) whether the short-term objectives have been achieved.

FURTHER READING

Brady, Shelly. *Ten Things I Learned from Bill Porter.* Novato, Calif.: New World Library, 2004.

Gale, editor. *Disabilites (Teen Rights and Freedoms).* Farmington Hills, Mich.: Greenhaven Press, 2014.

Huston, Todd, and Kay D. Rizzo. *More Than Mountains: The Todd Huston Story.* Nampa, Idaho: Pacific Press, 2005.

Stewart, Gail B. *Teens with Disabilities.* San Diego, Calif.: Lucent Books, 2001.

Thornton, Denise. *Physical Disabilities: The Ultimate Teen Guide.* Lanham, Md.: Scarecrow Press, 2012.

Whittaker, Tom. *Higher Purpose: The Heroic Story of the First Disabled Man to Conquer Everest.* Washington, D.C.: Lifeline Press, 2001.

FOR MORE INFORMATION

Ability OnLine
www.abilityonline.org

Amputee Coalition of America
www.amputee-coalition.org

Canadian Paralympic Committee
www.paralympic.ca

Muscular Dystrophy Association (MDA)
www.mdausa.org

The National Center on Physical Activity and Disability (NCPAD)
www.ncpad.org

National Dissemination Center for Children with Disabilities
www.nichcy.org

National Spinal Cord Injury Association
www.spinalcord.org

National Sports Center for the Disabled
www.nscd.org

Spina Bifida Association of America
www.sbaa.org

Publisher's Note:

The websites listed on these pages were active at the time of publication. The publisher is not responsible for websites that have changed their address or discontinued operation since the date of publication. The publisher will review and update the websites upon each reprint.

SERIES GLOSSARY OF KEY TERMS

Accessibility: An environment that allows people with disabilities to participate as much as they can.

Accommodation: A change in how a student receives instruction, without substantially changing the instructional content.

Achievement test: A standardized test that measures a student's performance in academic areas such as math, reading, and writing.

Acting out: Behavior that's inappropriate within the setting.

Adaptive behavior: The extent to which an individual is able to adjust to and apply new skills to new environments, tasks, objects, and people.

Ambulatory: Able to walk independently.

American Sign Language (ASL): A language based on gestures that is used by people who are deaf in the United States and Canada.

Americans with Disabilities Act (ADA): In 1990, Congress passed this act, which provides people who have disabilities with the same freedoms as Americans who do not have disabilities. The law addresses access to buildings and programs, as well as housing and employment.

Anxiety: An emotional state of fear, often not attached to any direct threat, which can cause sweating, increased pulse, and breathing difficulty.

Aphasia: Loss of the ability to speak.

Articulation: The ability to express oneself through sounds, words, and sentences.

Asperger syndrome: An disorder that is on the autism spectrum, which can cause problems with nonverbal learning disorder and social interactions.

Assessment: The process of collecting information about a student's learning needs through tests, observations, and interviewing the student, the family, and others. Assistive technology: Any item or piece of equipment that is used to improve the capabilities of a child with a disability.

Attention-deficit/hyperactivity Disorder (ADHD): A disorder that can cause inappropriate behavior, including poor attention skills, impulsivity, and hyperactivity.

Autism spectrum disorder: A range of disabilities that affect verbal and nonverbal communication and social interactions.

Bipolar disorder: A brain disorder that causes uncontrollable changes in moods, behaviors, thoughts, and activities.

Blind (legally): Visual acuity for distance vision of 20/200 or less in the better eye after best correction with conventional lenses; or a visual field of no greater than 20 degrees in the better eye.

Bullying: When a child faces threats, intimidation, name-calling, gossip, or physical violence.

Cerebral palsy (CP): Motor impairment caused by brain damage during birth or before birth. It can be mild to severe, does not get worse, and cannot be cured. Chronic: A condition that persists over a long period of time.

Cognitive: Having to do with remembering, reasoning, understanding, and using judgment.

Congenital: Any condition that is present at birth.

Counseling: Advice or help through talking, given by someone qualified to give such help.

Deaf: A hearing loss so severe that speech cannot be understood, even with a hearing aid, even if some sounds may still be perceived.

Developmental: Having to do with the steps or stages in growth and development of a child.

Disability: A limitation that interferes with a person's ability to walk, hear, talk, or learn.

Down syndrome: An abnormal chromosomal condition that changes the development of the body and brain, often causing intellectual disabilities.

Early intervention: Services provided to infants and toddlers ages birth to three who are at risk for or are showing signs of having a slower than usual development.

Emotional disturbance (ED): An educational term (rather than psychological) where a student's inability to build or maintain satisfactory interpersonal relationships with peers and teachers, inappropriate types of behavior or feelings, and moods of unhappiness or depression get in the way of the student being able to learn and function in a school setting.

Epilepsy: A brain disorder where the electrical signals in the brain are disrupted, causing seizures. Seizures can cause brief changes in a person's body movements, awareness, emotions, and senses (such as taste, smell, vision, or hearing).

Fine motor skills: Control of small muscles in the hands and fingers, which are needed for activities such as writing and cutting.

Gross motor skills: Control of large muscles in the arms, legs, and torso, which are needed for activities such as running and walking.

Hard-of-hearing: A hearing loss that may affect the student's educational performance.

Heredity: Traits acquired from parents.

Individualized Education Plan (IEP): A written education plan for students ages 5 to 22 with disabilities, developed by a team of professionals, (teachers, therapists, etc.) and the child's parent(s), which is reviewed and updated yearly. It contains a description of the child's level of development, learning needs, goals and objectives, and services the child will receive.

Individuals with Disabilities Education Act (IDEA): The Individuals with Disabilities Education Act (IDEA) is the nation's federal special education law that requires public schools to serve the educational needs of students with disabilities. IDEA requires that schools provide special education services to eligible students as outlined in a student's IEP, and it also provides very specific requirements to guarantee a free appropriate education for students with disabilities in the least restrictive environment.

Intervention: A planned activity to increase students' skills.

Learning disability: A general term for specific kinds of learning problems that can cause a person to have challenges learning and using certain skills, such as reading, writing, listening, speaking, reasoning, and doing math.

Least restrictive environment: The educational setting or program that provides a student with as much contact as possible with children without disabilities, while still appropriately meeting all of the child's learning and physical needs.

Mainstreaming: Providing any services, including education, for children with disabilities, in a setting with other children who do not have disabilities.

Motor: Having to do with muscular activity.

Nonambulatory: Not able to walk independently.

Occupational therapist (OT): A professional who helps individuals be able to handle meaningful activities of daily life such as self-care skills, education, recreation, work or social interaction.

Palate: The roof of the mouth.

Paraplegia: Paralysis of the legs and lower part of the body.

Partially sighted: A term formally used to indicate visual acuity of 20/70 to 20/200, but also used to describe visual impairment in which usable vision is present.

Pediatrics: The medical treatment of children.

Physical therapist (PT): A person who helps individuals improve the use of bones, muscles, joints, and/or nerves.

Prenatal: Existing or occurring prior to birth.

Quadriplegia: Paralysis affecting all four limbs.

Referral: In special education, students are referred for screening and evaluation to see if they are eligible for special education services.

Self-care skills: The ability to care for oneself; usually refers to basic habits of dressing, eating, etc.

Special Education: Specialized instruction made to fit the unique learning strengths and needs of each student with disabilities in the least restrictive environment.

Speech impaired: Communication disorder such as stuttering, impaired articulation, a language impairment, or a voice impairment, which adversely affects a child's educational performance.

Speech pathologist: A trained therapist, who provides treatment to help a person develop or improve articulation, communication skills, and oral-motor skills.

Spina bifida: A problem that happens in the first month of pregnancy when the spinal column doesn't close completely.

Standardized tests: Tests that use consistent directions, procedures, and criteria for scoring, which are often administered to many students in many schools across the country.

Stereotyping: A generalization in which individuals are falsely assigned traits they do not possess based on race, ethnicity, religion, disability, or gender.

Symptom: An observable sign of an illness or disorder.

Syndrome: A set of symptoms that occur together.

Therapy: The treatment or application of different techniques to improve specific conditions for curing or helping to live with various disorders.

Traumatic Brain Injury (TBI): Physical damage to the brain that could result in physical, behavioral, or mental changes depending on which area of the brain is injured.

Visually impaired: Any degree of vision loss that affects an individual's ability to perform the tasks of daily life, which is caused by a visual system that is not working properly or not formed correctly.

Vocational education: Educational programs that prepare students for paid or unpaid employment, or which provide additional preparation for a career that doesn't require a college degree.

INDEX

ABOUT THE AUTHOR
AND THE CONSULTANTS

Joan Esherick is a full-time author, freelance writer, and professional speaker who has a son with physical challenges. Her recent books include *Our Mighty Fortress: Finding Refuge in God* (Moody Press, 2002), and multiple books in Mason Crest's THE STATE OF MENTAL ILLNESS AND ITS THERAPY series and their LIVING WITH A SPECIAL NEED series. She has contributed dozens of articles to national periodicals and speaks nationwide.

Dr. Lisa Albers is a developmental behavioral pediatrician at Children's Hospital Boston and Harvard Medical School, where her responsibilities include outpatient pediatric teaching and patient care in the Developmental Medicine Center. She currently is Director of the Adoption Program, Director of Fellowships in Developmental and Behavioral Pediatrics, and collaborates in a consultation program for community health centers. She is also the school consultant for the Walker School, a residential school for children in the state foster care system.

Dr. Carolyn Bridgemohan is an instructor in pediatrics at Harvard Medical School and is a board-certified developmental behavioral pediatrician on staff in the Developmental Medicine Center at Children's Hospital, Boston. Her clinical practice includes children and youth with autism, hearing impairment, developmental language disorders, global delays, intellectual disabilities, and attention and learning disorders. Dr. Bridgemohan is coeditor of *Bright Futures Case Studies for Primary Care Clinicians: Child Development and Behavior*, a curriculum used nationwide in pediatric residency training programs.

Cindy Croft is the State Special Needs Director in Minnesota, coordinating Project EXCEPTIONAL MN, through Concordia University. Project EXCEPTIONAL MN is a state project that supports the inclusion of children in community settings through training, on-site consultation, and professional development. She also teaches as adjunct faculty for Concordia University, St. Paul, Minnesota. She has worked in the special needs arena for the past fifteen years.

Dr. Laurie Glader is a developmental pediatrician at Children's Hospital in Boston where she directs the Cerebral Palsy Program and is a staff pediatrician with the Coordinated Care Services, a program designed to meet the needs of children with special health care needs. Dr. Glader also teaches regularly at Harvard Medical School. Her work with public agencies includes New England SERVE, an organization that builds connections between state health departments, health care organizations, community providers, and families. She is also the staff physician at the Cotting School, a school specializing in the education of children with a wide range of special health care needs.